WD

2.

ISSUES THAT CONCERN YOU

Prejudice

Crystal McCage, *Book Editor*

GREENHAVEN PRESS

A part of Gale, Cengage Learning

GALE
CENGAGE Learning

Detroit • New York • San Francisco • New Haven, Conn • Waterville, Maine • London

Christine Nasso, *Publisher*
Elizabeth Des Chenes, *Managing Editor*

© 2009 Greenhaven Press, a part of Gale, Cengage Learning

Gale and Greenhaven Press are registered trademarks used herein under license.

For more information, contact:
Greenhaven Press
27500 Drake Rd.
Farmington Hills, MI 48331-3535
Or you can visit our Internet site at gale.cengage.com

For product information and technology assistance, contact us at

Gale Customer Support, 1-800-877-4253
For permission to use material from this text or product, submit all requests online at
www.cengage.com/permissions

Further permissions questions can be emailed to permissionrequest@cengage.com

Articles in Greenhaven Press anthologies are often edited for length to meet page requirements. In addition, original titles of these works are changed to clearly present the main thesis and to explicitly indicate the author's opinion. Every effort is made to ensure that Greenhaven Press accurately reflects the original intent of the authors. Every effort has been made to trace the owners of copyrighted material.

Cover image copyright MalibuBooks, 2009. Used under license from Shutterstock.com

LIBRARY OF CONGRESS CATALOGING-IN-PUBLICATION DATA

Prejudice / Crystal McCage, book editor.
   p. cm. -- (Issues that concern you)
 Includes bibliographical references and index.
 ISBN 978-0-7377-4349-4 (hardcover)
1. Prejudices--Juvenile literature. I. McCage, Crystal.
 HM1091.P74 2009
 303.3'85--dc22

                                     2008051755

Printed in the United States of America
1 2 3 4 5 6 7 13 12 11 10 09

3 9957 00147 4705

CONTENTS

Prejudice is essentially any negative attitude held by a member of one group of people toward another group. Typically, people are subjected to prejudice because of their race, ethnicity, religion, gender, or sexual orientation. In the United States, people in these categories—with sexual orientation being the exception in many cases—are protected from discrimination in schools, the workplace, and elsewhere by the rights spelled out in laws and in the U.S. Constitution.

While institutional prejudice can be protected against, personal prejudices are more subtle and harder to combat. For example, research has shown that persons responsible for hiring decisions have unconscious prejudices that influence them. One study showed that employers made assumptions that people who spoke with a Southern accent were less intelligent than those who did not. Because such prejudices are often unconscious, they are difficult to change.

Many studies have attempted to determine the origins of prejudicial attitudes. Some such attitudes are definitely learned. Children raised in a household where parents dislike a particular minority, for example, grow up hearing disparaging comments about that minority. They may then find themselves believing what their parents believe. The same is true of the influence of peer groups: A young person may absorb the beliefs of an influential friend and begin expressing such beliefs as his or her own.

New research, however, is showing that prejudice may also be an innate part of the human brain. Essentially, humans may categorize other humans into groups without thinking about it. This response may have helped early humans survive by enabling them to determine quickly who was an enemy and who was a friend. Although this research sheds light on the origins of prejudice, it does not offer a justification for prejudicial behavior. People can clearly learn to overcome prejudice, whatever its origins.

In a display of prejudice, the Ku Klux Klan burns a cross, showing their enmity toward African Americans.

Most people agree that prejudice must be actively discouraged, but vigorous debate has arisen over the question of how best to do so. Some believe prejudice is best addressed through legislation, such as affirmative action programs that actively recruit minorities and women into the workplace, and educational institutions. Others believe that education and awareness can effectively combat prejudice. Many schools in the United States present multicultural curricula and diversity training programs to make students aware of prejudice and to discuss ways that prejudice can be minimized.

These combined efforts may be working. In a 2007 poll, the vast majority of Americans expressed a willingness to vote for either a woman or a minority presidential candidate. In 2008 Barack Obama made history as the first black major-party presidential candidate in the United States. Then, on November 8, 2008, Obama broke long-standing political and social barriers by becoming the first black president in U.S. history. This development would have been unheard of even fifty years ago in the United States.

Understanding prejudice is essential to a pluralistic society, one in which people of varying cultures and beliefs coexist in an atmosphere of mutual respect and cooperation. The authors featured in *Issues That Concern You: Prejudice* explore many facts of the issue, examining various causes and examples of prejudice as well as potential solutions for reducing or eliminating prejudicial attitudes and actions.

In addition, the volume includes a bibliography, a list of organizations to contact for further information, and other useful appendixes. The appendix titled "What You Should Know About Prejudice" offers vital facts about prejudice and how it affects young people. The appendix "What You Should Do About Prejudice" discusses various solutions to the problem of discrimination. These many useful features make *Issues That Concern You: Prejudice* a valuable resource. Given the growing costs of prejudice to society, having a greater understanding of this issue is critical.

ONE

Prejudice Is Real in the United States

Steve Coll

> The roots of racial tension run deep in the South. In the following article Steve Coll uses a school in Jena, Louisiana, as a launching point for arguing that prejudice remains deeply rooted in the American South. Coll concludes that just being black places one at a disadvantage in many ways in the United States. Coll is a Pulitzer Prize–winning journalist and managing editor of *The Washington Post*.

Just over a year ago, during a high-school assembly in Jena, Louisiana, a black student asked the school's white principal if it would be all right to sit under an oak tree outside, an oasis of shade known as the "white tree," because only Caucasian students congregated there. The principal said that the young man could sit where he liked. Later, the student and some African-American friends walked over to the oak and chatted with some white schoolmates. The next day, somebody fixed two nooses to the tree's branches.

The ropes inaugurated a narrative of conflict and small-town justice in the Deep South known today as the case of the Jena Six, a story populated by a disconcerting number of stock characters from the late Jim Crow era. Its origins signaled a theatrical quality that a swelling cast, including the Reverend Al Sharpton, has managed to sustain; an Off Broadway production (backlit oak tree, gentle wind machines, soliloquies about past and present) seems inevitable.

Although some of the evidence in the Jena case is murky, a cumulative verdict of racial double standards lies beyond reasonable doubt. Between Reconstruction and the end of the Second World War, more than two hundred and fifty people in Louisiana, the great majority of them African-Americans, were lynched. Jena's recent noosemakers, identified as a trio of white students, were recommended for expulsion by the principal, who was evidently conscious of this history, but a white school superintendent imposed suspensions only, on the ground that the tree display was a prank. In the days leading up to that decision, fights had erupted between black and white students, and the local district attorney, Reed Walters, reportedly gave a speech in which he warned students, "With a stroke of my pen, I can make your lives disappear."

Last December, at the school, a black student coldcocked a white student, Justin Barker, knocking him briefly unconscious; other black students allegedly kicked the victim while he lay on the ground. Barker was treated for cuts and bruises at a hospital and released a few hours later. The police arrested six black students, aged fourteen to eighteen, and Walters charged them with attempted second-degree murder and a conspiracy count; if convicted, they faced up to seventy-five years in prison.

Jena prosecutors started reducing the charges to aggravated second-degree battery and conspiracy. Still, last June an all-white jury convicted one of the defendants, Mychal Bell, who was sixteen years old at the time of the assault, of crimes that threatened him with up to twenty-two years in an adult state prison. Michael Baisden, a black syndicated radio talk-show host who normally specializes in romance and its perils, undertook an on-air protest, along with others, which spread across black radio and then to the Internet. In late September, thousands of demonstrators descended on Jena. Last Thursday, Bell, whose convictions had been thrown out, was released on bail, after

Widespread protests against the Jena Six convictions in Jena, Louisiana, were sparked by the Internet and black radio.

ten months in jail; Reed Walters has agreed to retry him as a juvenile.

Last week, in the *Times*, Walters defended his work; he described himself as just "a lawyer obligated to enforce the laws of my state." A devotion to the sanctity of statutes is, of course, essential in a nation governed by laws, but equally important is the exercise of prosecutorial discretion, derived from an intuitive commitment to fairness and common sense. If Walters had possessed a modest measure of such judgment, he might have rescued himself and the town of Jena from notoriety many months ago.

His bullheadedness, however, does not explain why Jena's narrative has resonated so broadly. Many African-Americans understand the case not only as the civil-rights era redux but as a stark illustration of a here-and-now problem, one about which whites are mainly silent: the mass incarceration of black youths—America's "school-to-prison pipeline," as some scholars have christened it.

The number of blacks in prison has quadrupled since 1980. There are many overlapping causes, among them severe automated federal sentencing rules; a passionate but badly managed "war on drugs" prosecuted most heavily in African-American neighborhoods; and deepening inequalities in personal income and access to education, whose effects fall hardest on urban teenagers. One study estimates that, if recent trends continue, a third of the black males born in 2001 can expect to do time.

The state of Louisiana, true to its reputation for rococo extremism in all matters political, locks up in prison a higher percentage of its population—black, white, and all other races combined—than any other state in the nation. It might be of some comfort to politicians, then, if the Jena case, like the disgraceful treatment of displaced African-American victims of Hurricane Katrina, could be rationalized as an isolated, swamp-inspired exception to a more temperate American norm.

The opposite is true, however. In July, the Sentencing Project, a research and advocacy group, released a state-by-state study of prison populations that identified where blacks endured the highest rates of incarceration. The top four states were South Dakota, Wisconsin, Iowa, and Vermont; the top ten included Utah, Montana, and Colorado—not places renowned for their African-American subcultures. In the United States today, driving while black—or shoplifting while black, or taking illegal drugs, or hitting schoolmates—often carries the greatest risk of incarceration, in comparison to the risk faced by whites, in states where people of color are rare, including a few states that are liberal, prosperous, and not a little self-satisfied. Ex-slave states that are relatively poor and have large African-American populations, such as Louisiana, display less racial disparity.

Discrimination in the American justice system is not only a Deep South thing; it is a national embarrassment. [French historian

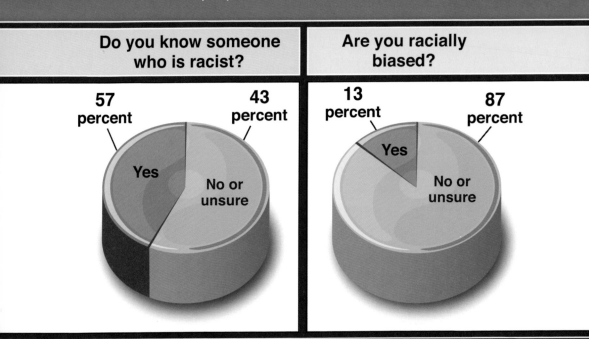

Most Americans See Racism in Others

A recent CNN poll shows that most Americans have a hard time seeing racism in themselves yet can identify it in others. When asked if they knew someone whom they thought was racist, 43 percent of whites said yes. However, just 13 percent of whites considered themselves racially biased. Researchers stress that these numbers indicate that people are blind to their own biases.

Do you know someone who is racist?

57 percent — Yes

43 percent — No or unsure

Are you racially biased?

13 percent — Yes

87 percent — No or unsure

Taken from: CNN poll, "Most Americans See Lingering Racism—in Others," 2006. www.cnn.com.

and political writer Alexis de] Tocqueville, who initially came to America to study its penal system, might wonder how a democracy can so earnestly debate the justice of detaining foreign nationals at Guantánamo while displaying not a whiff of discomfort about the record number of its own citizens—now more than two million—stuffed into jails and prisons, or about the causes of racial disparity in this forgotten population. America's predominant response to racism, of course, has long been denial. In Jena, the town fathers effected a vivid evasion. Their problem, they concluded, was not themselves but their tree: they cut down the offending oak and hauled it away.

TWO

Prejudice Is Often Unconscious

Chris de Morsella

> Chris de Morsella is chief operating officer of the Multicultural Advantage, a Web site that provides resources on diversity in the workplace and diversity recruiting effectiveness for companies. In this viewpoint Morsella points out that subconscious prejudices can be harmful. He argues that awareness of prejudice is the important first step in doing something about it.

Even though implicit prejudice may arise from below our level of awareness it still has a very real impact on our behavior, on how we view others and act towards them. As long as it remains hidden within the unconscious and is ignored by society it will continue to act upon us in a negative manner. It is little comfort to the victims of prejudice that the prejudice was probably unconscious. It still means that they are unfairly passed over for promotions, refused interviews based on their names, denied bank loans, and refused opportunities to view homes they want to purchase.

Prejudice that is implicit still has the same harmful effect as prejudice which is consciously practiced to those who suffer because of it. It is a very real problem to the people it affects, even if those, whose attitudes and actions are influenced by it may be unaware themselves of the nature of their behavior and their attitudes.

Chris de Morsella, "Implicit Prejudice Unconsciously Colors Our World," The Multicultural Advantage, 2007. Reproduced by author's permission. www.multiculturaladvantage.com.

What Can Be Done to Combat Implicit Prejudice?

Some may be asking themselves: How can we know it exists or measure it if it arises from the unconscious? Unconscious attitudes and stereotypes can be teased out into the open by a technique that relies on measuring how test subjects respond to associations of value-laden words with visual images. Computer-based implicit association tests (IAT) can reveal the presence of this kind of unconscious prejudice within test subjects. These kinds of tests, first developed by University of Washington professor Anthony Greenwald, measure split-second differentials in reaction times to a series of associative memory questions that pair value laden word phrases with visual stimuli. For example, computer programs assess the degree to which people associate positive and negative words with different ethnic groups.

Harvard's Project Implicit has found that ordinary people sometimes have negative associations toward particular groups even though they report having no such biases.

Testing for implicit prejudice is a controversial subject with some critics maintaining that these types of tests do not really measure unconscious prejudice, but only harmless cultural knowledge. However a meta-analysis by Greenwald and [Mahzarin] Banaji across 61 studies has shown that IAT test results predicted judgments, opinions and behavior linked to stereotyping and prejudice better than expressed attitudes could. This conclusion is also backed up by other studies, including a University of Colorado study published in the *Journal of Personality and Social Psychology* in 1997: "Evidence for Racial Prejudice at the Implicit Level and Its Relationship With Questionnaire Measures" by Bernd Wittenbrink, Charles M. Judd, and Bernadette Park.

At Harvard's Project Implicit web site you can test yourself on 14 different measures of implicit prejudice and find out if you automatically favor people with light skin over dark skin or young over old, for example. Even genuinely egalitarian people may find that the test results reveal a hidden prejudice that they are not aware of, a prejudice that arises from below the level of our awareness.

Discovering the existence of unconscious stereotypic attitudes within ourselves can be an unsettling experience especially for those of us who on a conscious level see themselves as being mostly free of prejudicial behavior. However it also has the potential to help us look into ourselves and begin the process of disentangling who we consciously choose to be from these hidden signaling systems that lie buried beneath our awareness. By becoming aware of our own implicit prejudices, we can help our conscious attitudes take charge.

As social psychologist Mahzarin Banaji of the Harvard faculty says in "Making case for concept of 'implicit prejudice,'" "We've found that ordinary people, including ourselves, harbor negative associations toward particular social groups on 'implicit' measures of bias, even though they honestly report having no such bias at the conscious level," says Banaji. And this bias is hardly inconsequential, she says: Implicit attitudes, they have found, predict behavior, from simple acts of friendliness and inclusion to judgments of "goodness" or evaluation of the quality of work.

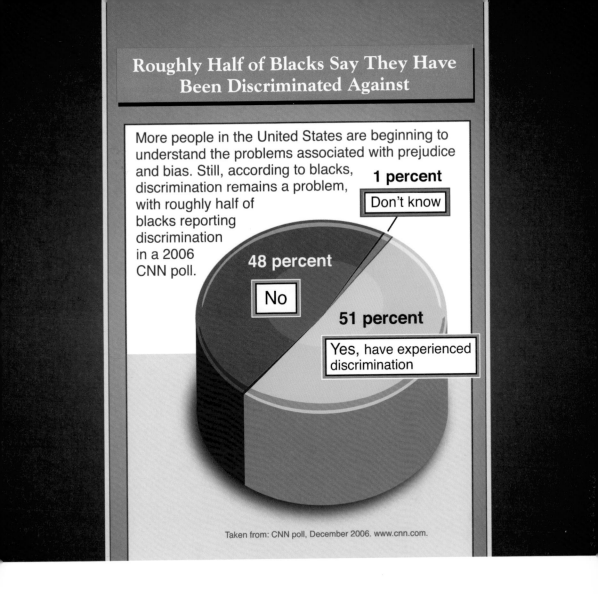

Roughly Half of Blacks Say They Have Been Discriminated Against

More people in the United States are beginning to understand the problems associated with prejudice and bias. Still, according to blacks, discrimination remains a problem, with roughly half of blacks reporting discrimination in a 2006 CNN poll.

1 percent

Don't know

48 percent

No

51 percent

Yes, have experienced discrimination

Taken from: CNN poll, December 2006. www.cnn.com.

Prejudice Can Be Overcome

It is fair to say that all of us form our conscious views based, at least partially, on unconscious processes of which we are consciously unaware. This is how our brains work and in many cases this rapid fire means of arriving at a judgment or adopting an attitude may be harmless or even very beneficial. Certainly it played an important role in our survival in our natural prehistorical habitat, much as the shadow of a hawk's wing causes a rabbit to run for cover. However, when the unexamined mind leads us to behave in a manner that is harmful to others we should shine the light of self-examination onto the hidden processes that lie within and that generate the ill behavior.

There's no way to wipe out all the years of evolution during which humans and their ancestors learned to fear the unfamiliar, to be ready to flee from or fight at any threat. But fortunately our brains are flexible enough to be altered by experience. Much in the same way that we consciously can break a bad-eating habit, for example, by catching ourselves when we reach for the junk food without thinking and consciously habituating ourselves to eat healthier foods, we can also consciously address these hidden prejudices that color our worlds. The first step in doing so, is becoming aware that we may in fact have what Mahzarin Banaji has termed—using jargon borrowed from the world of computer programming—mind bug or mistakes in perception that give rise to unconscious forms of prejudice.

THREE

Prejudice May Be Physiological

Robert Burton

> Author Robert Burton is the former chief of neurology
> at Mount Zion University of California at San Francisco
> Hospital. Burton overviews new research on the brain
> that indicates prejudice is natural in human beings and
> explains how our brains group and classify. This research
> contradicts assertions that prejudice is learned. However,
> he asserts that, while we should not pretend we are free
> from bias, it is not acceptable to act on that bias. Burton
> argues that when we are aware of our prejudices we can
> still make moral decisions about how to treat others.

I am stuck in rush-hour traffic. Maybe I can find a decent radio
program to distract myself from the blasting horns, angry looks
and cussing behind rolled-up windows. But the radio is worse than
the traffic. On NPR, a Washington think tank guru is arguing
that "my 30-plus years of studying the Middle East has convinced
me that democracy is more appropriate for some cultures than
others." A second NPR station is airing a debate on the medical
rights of "illegal aliens." On Fox, Bill O'Reilly is talking about
a recent dinner in Harlem, N.Y., with Al Sharpton: "I couldn't
get over the fact that there was no difference between Sylvia's

Robert Burton, "We're Prejudiced, Now What?" *Salon*, October 31, 2007. This article first
appeared in *Salon* at www.salon.com. An online version remains in the *Salon* archives. Reprinted
with permission.

restaurant and any other restaurant in New York City. I mean, it was exactly the same, even though it's run by blacks."

Social Science Struggles to Explain Prejudice

Everywhere I turn, someone is honking at the other guy. Once upon a time, when psychology was king of the behavioral hill, I thought that prejudice could be explained by upbringing, cultural influences, socioeconomic disparities and plain old wrong thinking. Despite any hard evidence from soft sciences, I nursed the vaguely optimistic belief that education and the teaching of tolerance might make a dent in the bigotry and racism of "others." And yet sitting in stalled traffic, I cannot shake the irrational feeling that "those in the other cars" are different from "us in our car." If my mind seems intent upon making such ludicrous and meaningless distinctions, is there more here than meets the purely psychological I?

Psychologists have long talked about our tendency to form "in groups" based upon skin color, accents (the Parisian vs. the "country French") and hairstyle (try to look at green spiked hair and a crew cut without drawing inferences of fundamental differences in personality). In his 1954 book, *The Nature of Prejudice*, psychologist Gordon Allport observed that many white Americans live in a "state of conflict." On one hand, they may be ideologically opposed to prejudice, but on the other, they possess underlying tendencies to think and act in racially biased ways.

Neuroscience Offers a New Explanation

Neuroscience is now providing tantalizing hints as to how these tendencies might occur. In 2000, two fMRI (functional magnetic resonance imaging) studies allowed the first visualizations of the underlying neuroanatomy of prejudice. In one study, Allan Hart, an Amherst social psychologist, found that when white and black subjects were given brief subliminal glimpses of faces of the other race, both showed increased activity in the amygdala, a small set of nuclei within the medial temporal lobes, believed to be responsible for processing the emotional significance of a stimulus.

In his groundbreaking 1954 book, The Nature of Prejudice, *Dr. Gordon Allport observed that people may be against prejudice, but they also possess underlying tendencies to think and act in racially biased ways.*

In a separate study, New York University neuroscientist Elizabeth Phelps found that the degree of increased amygdala activity directly correlated with both physiological and psychological testing evidence for prejudiced responses. Most important, these biased subjects were unaware of having seen the faces or of having any emotional response. Based upon these and subsequent confirming studies, the amygdala is now thought to be integral to the biology of unconscious discrimination.

Given that the amygdala has long been recognized to be instrumental in emotional processing, particularly in relationship to learning, perception and expression of fear, it has seemed reasonable to interpret such studies as showing that viewing different-colored skin might trigger fear or apprehension. However, Phelps and others have cautioned that the amygdala also responds more generally to the emotional intensity of a stimulus—not only fear but also ambiguity, vigilance and even some states of uncertainty that can have a positive outcome. So, given our present state of knowledge, fMRI activation of the amygdala should not be taken as unequivocal evidence that the fear and anxiety are the primary unconscious responses to racial or ethnic differences; the activation could represent a nonspecific state of heightened emotional arousal.

Naturally, evolutionary biologists are quick to point out the obvious adaptive benefits of immediate unconscious recognition of any difference that might indicate a potential enemy or predator. UCLA [University of California at Los Angeles] anthropologist Rob Boyd has written extensively that being attuned to ethnic differences allows individuals to identify others who share the same cultural norms; sharing similar expectations makes social interaction a lot easier than mixing it up with those with different expectations.

At an equally basic neural level, reflexive detection of differences is an essential aspect of how we learn through pattern recognition. For example, the brain contains primary modules for distinguishing colors. These neural systems operate outside of awareness. One cannot choose not to see a color difference. Even at a young age, such differences contribute to our worldview. According to studies by University of Michigan psychologist Lawrence Hirschfeld, 3-year-old children already attribute significance to skin color and appear to believe that race is the most important physical characteristic in determining what sort of person one is.

Innate Tendencies to Be Prejudiced

The evidence is pouring in; at bottom, we seem programmed to seek out and create meaning out of perceived differences. The question that continues to hound me: Is it possible to break this cycle of prejudgment?

A relatively new and utterly intriguing approach to seeing how prejudice may have evolved and taken root in our brains is "agent-based computational modeling." This imposing mouthful is nothing more than a clever description of using computers to study how complex systems arise out of basic elements. The technique is relatively straightforward. You create tiny computer programs (agents) with only a few sets of instructions. You then place them on a computer grid and watch their interactions over thousands of trial periods.

Such computer models are now commonly used to predict such disparate activities as consumer behavior, seasonal migration of birds, sexual reproduction, the transmission of diseases and even how culture spreads and becomes established. In evolutionary models, individual characteristics and behavioral strategies can be followed over multiple generations to see how successful behaviors gradually gain dominance. It is presumed that, over time, the optimal strategy for survival will emerge from initially random encounters.

Using this technique, University of Michigan political scientist Robert Axelrod and his colleague Ross Hammond of the Brookings Institution in Washington, D.C., have studied how ethnocentric behavior may have evolved even in the absence of any initial bias or prejudice. To make the model as simple as possible, they made each agent one of four possible colors. None of the colors was given any positive or negative ranking with respect to the other colors; in the beginning, all colors were created equal. The agents were then provided with instructions (simple algorithms) as to possible ways to respond when encountering another agent. One algorithm specified whether or not the agent cooperated when meeting someone of its own color. The other algorithm specified whether or not the agent cooperated with agents of a different color.

The scientists defined an ethnocentric strategy as one in which an agent cooperated only with other agents of its own color, and not with agents of other colors. The other strategies were to cooperate with everyone, cooperate with no one and cooperate only with agents of a different color. Since only one of the four possible strategies is ethnocentric and all were equally likely, random interactions would result in a 25 percent rate of ethnocentric behavior. Yet their studies consistently demonstrated that greater than three-fourths of the agents eventually adopted an ethnocentric strategy. In short, although the agents weren't programmed to have any initial bias for or against any color, they gradually evolved an ethnocentric preference for one's own color at the expense of those of another color.

Axelrod and Hammond don't claim that their studies duplicate the real-world complexities of prejudice and discrimination. But it is hard to ignore that an initially meaningless trait morphed into a trigger for group bias. Contrary to how most of us see bigotry and prejudice as arising out of faulty education and early-childhood indoctrination, Axelrod's model doesn't begin with preconceived notions about the relative values of different colors, nor is it associated with any underlying negative emotional state such as envy, frustration or animosity. Detection of a difference, no matter how innocent, is enough to result in ethnocentric strategies.

Even more striking, there isn't any conventional "thought" associated with this prejudice; it emerges in the same way as ants build ant colonies, and cities and societies form without prior planning or specific intention. Nowhere in the agent's minuscule "mind" is there any line of code on how best to proceed; there is no built-in suggestion that discrimination might provide better rates of reproduction or survival.

In "The Selfish Gene," Richard Dawkins said in his characteristic blunt manner, "We are survival machines—robot vehicles blindly programmed to preserve the selfish molecules known as genes." No matter how inflammatory Dawkins' rhetoric might sound, his observation is consistent with the conclusions of Axelrod's agent-modeling studies.

So is this powerful self-interest strategy truly in the genes, and even if it is, can it be modified by experience and education? It's clear that ethnocentricity is the optimal strategy when mutual distrust is the default position between different groups. But a variety of game theory simulations, like the prisoner's dilemma, designed to study cooperation vs. noncooperation between two people or groups, suggest that under certain circumstances, mutual cooperation is the preferable strategy.

In a worldwide competition held by Axelrod, academics were asked to create a variety of programs for how agents might best interact for long-term survival. The winner was a simple program, tit for tat, which specified that an agent would always cooperate with another agent at their first encounter; after that, one agent would adopt whatever strategy the opponent demonstrated. If the other guy (agent) responds favorably to your initial offer, cooperation ensues. If the opponent rejects cooperation, you abandon niceness and revert to mutual mistrust. Tit for tat showed that a single attempt at cooperation, prior to knowing how the other agent would respond, resulted in a better long-term outcome for both agents. Trust, in other words, is good.

If such computer simulations are applicable to human behavior, the moral is transparently frustrating. In meeting someone perceived as being different, we must offer initial trust and cooperation without any guarantee that the other person will reciprocate. But anyone who has resolved to adopt the doctrine of unilateral compassion and "turn the other cheek" knows how difficult such self-sacrificing behavior is to initiate unilaterally.

The encouraging news: Axelrod has used such studies to show how cooperative behavior can evolve from mechanisms that, by natural selection, are inherently selfish. The not-so-good news: It isn't at all clear how humans can overcome basic emotions such as fear, anger, the urge for retribution or just a heightened emotional arousal that make initial cooperation so antithetical to how we normally react to perceived differences.

Bias Must Be Acknowledged to Be Avoided

Nevertheless, Elizabeth Phelps has repeatedly emphasized that the behavioral studies demonstrating unconscious bias "do not indicate that this behavior is 'hard-wired,' or unchangeable." In her 2000 study, she demonstrated that our unconscious biased

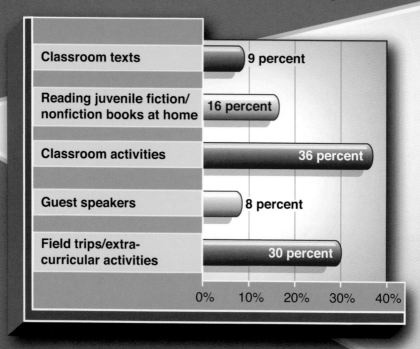

Parents Say Diversity Awareness Can Be Taught in a Variety of Ways

In a recent online poll of about one thousand parents, most said that classroom and extracurricular activities were the best ways for their children to learn about diversity issues.

Classroom texts	9 percent
Reading juvenile fiction/ nonfiction books at home	16 percent
Classroom activities	36 percent
Guest speakers	8 percent
Field trips/extra- curricular activities	30 percent

0%   10%   20%   30%   40%

Taken from: Family Education, "Diversity Education," August 2008. www.familyeducation.com.

responses (amygdala activation) can be significantly reduced by experience and familiarity. In other words, emergent prejudiced behavior isn't an inescapable aspect of our biology.

Admittedly, one of the greatest obstacles to a frank discussion of bias is the repugnance of prejudice. As ugly traits go, racist and bigot are right up there with pedophile and cannibal. But somehow we need to get over our puritanical revulsion with aspects of our biology that we find morally unacceptable. Being politically correct and denying the presence of unconscious bias has been shown to have its own downside. In a clever fMRI study, psychologist Jennifer Richeson has demonstrated that trying not to have inappropriate racial thoughts can actually tax brain activity and result in lesser performance on psychological tests that require maximal attention and concentration.

There's no doubt that ethnocentric philosophies can be deliberate attempts to justify everything from eugenics to xenophobia. But cognitive science is also showing how many of our thoughts begin outside of awareness. It isn't much of a leap to believe that conscious thoughts, including racist or ethnocentric beliefs, are after-the-fact rationalizations for unconscious behaviors that have survival benefits. (In fMRI studies, activation of the amygdala corresponded with the subjects making racially biased decisions, despite being unaware of feeling any bias.) If so, we shouldn't be surprised that the most cogent arguments against discrimination rarely shake biased beliefs.

For me, real bigotry begins with the hubris and arrogance of those like Bill O'Reilly who insist that their assessment of others is purely based upon reason and conscious deliberation, as opposed to being colored by involuntary and unrecognized elements of prejudice. For us to treat others with real trust, we must begin by acknowledging our biases and consciously doing the hard mental work to overcome them. We may not be able to prevent biased opinions from arising, but we do retain the veto power over whether to believe in and act on them.

We are left with two options. We can pretend we are free of bias, and avoid thinking about how to deal with our own deeply ingrained tendency to discriminate. Or we can take a lesson from neuroscience, and even from dumb computer agents, which can switch from noncooperation to cooperation if they learn that it is in their best interests.

FOUR

Women Still Face Prejudice in the Workplace

Harriet Rubin

In the following viewpoint author and journalist Harriet Rubin argues that sexism in the workplace continues in America, even though many believe that women and men are treated equally. Rubin cites recent research indicating a backslide in the progress women made in American businesses and points out that sexism is a real issue to be dealt with in American corporations.

Thirty years ago, two Harvard Business School professors had a plan. They wanted to change the world. Start filling the pipeline with female managers, they predicted, and in 10 or 20 years at most, those women would shift into senior positions. Once that took place, could an end to sexism in the workplace (and maybe everywhere else too) be far off? Anne Jardim and her partner, Margaret Hennig, wrote one of the first books of career advice for pigeonholed secretaries and ambitious assistants: *The Managerial Woman.* . . .

When it was published, in 1977, just 2.3 percent of the executives in U.S. firms were women. The book—a "groundbreaking" bestseller, according to the *New York Times*—was onto something big. Now, three decades later, 52 percent of all middle managers are women.

Poof! Sexism in corporate America—gone.

Harriet Rubin, "Sexism," Portfolio.com, April 2008. Reproduced by permission of the author and Writers Representatives LLC.

Sexism Is Still an Issue

Twenty or 30 years ago, people thought it could actually work like that: Deal with sexism and be done with it. . . . But sexism didn't end. Now we dread having to bring it up again. Why? Maybe because our failure stirs up fear and embarrassment at the idea that it will never go away. These thoughts are always with us but never more so than today, thanks to Senator Hillary Clinton's tumultuous presidential campaign. She was the "inevitable" Democratic candidate—until she wasn't. Once there was a charismatic male contender, we as a nation had to once again face our true feelings about gender and power. Suddenly the question is whether we are more gender-blind or color-blind.

Consider this: While women have made huge professional gains in the past three decades, progress now appears to have slowed or stalled. In some cases, it's even backsliding. Key indicators such as pay, board seats, and corporate-officer posts all reflect a leveling off or drop in recent years. Although the gap between men's and women's pay narrowed significantly through the 1980s, gains since then have been partly erased by a drop every few years. In 2006, women over the age of 25 earned 78.7 cents for every dollar earned by men, according to the most recent statistics from the U.S. Labor Department. That's a decline from 2005's figure of 79.4 cents on the dollar and also represents only about a 5-cent increase since 1991.

In the legal profession, the American Bar Association says the salaries of female lawyers are slipping in comparison with those of their male colleagues. Again according to the most recent statistics available, female attorneys' weekly wages amounted to 70.5 percent of male lawyers' in 2006, compared with 77.5 percent in 2005.

Among Fortune 500 firms, the number of female officers has declined each year since 2005, following substantial gains in the past decade. Sixty-four firms had zero female officers in 2006; last year [2007] the tally was 74, according to Catalyst, a nonprofit research and advisory organization that focuses on professional women. During the same period, the number of corporations with three or more female officers dropped from 234 to 203.

Despite the fact that many believe that women and men are treated equally in the workplace, recent research has shown that workplace sexism is still a pervasive issue.

Slowed Progress

In the early and mid-1990s, the number of female appointees to Fortune 500 boards steadily increased. But since then, progress has slowed, and it stalled last year: In 2007, women held 14.8 percent of board seats in Fortune 500 companies. And some of the companies thought to be the coolest are the most shamelessly female-averse: Apple has one female board member, appointed just this year [2008]; Microsoft has one; and Google has two. A Microsoft spokesperson said, "We are proud of the makeup of our board of directors. Microsoft is sensitive to diversity and inclusion; it continues to be an ongoing area of focus across the company. Board membership will always be based on the qualifications and perspective that the people we're considering can bring to the company's business and shareholders."

Heidrick & Struggles is one of the world's top executive-search firms. Senior chairman and chief headhunter Gerry Roche groaned when I told him why I was calling. "There isn't sexism anymore," he said. "Or if there is, you can't rush things. Maybe it will take another generation to make things right."

He told me, "Boards are always asking me to bring them women candidates." But he still places nearly six times as many men as women. Of his top 10 recruiters, five are female. So why only one woman on his nine-person board? "That's a good question," he said.

Catalyst calculates that, at this rate, it will take 73 years for women to achieve parity with men at the board level. 2081, here we come!

FIVE

America Is More Sexist than Racist

Drake Bennett

Drake Bennett is a journalist and staff writer for *The Boston Globe*. In the following article he reports on research suggesting that Americans struggle more with sexism than racism. According to the research, gender stereotypes seem to be strong among Americans, something that Bennett says did not help Senator Hillary Clinton in her 2008 presidential campaign. Bennett points out that research indicates that racial stereotyping is highly contextual and can be reversed more easily than gender stereotyping.

S ince Barack Obama emerged as a serious challenger to Hillary Clinton for the Democratic presidential nomination, the primaries have become, in part, a referendum on whether Americans are more prepared for a woman or a black man in the White House. The voting has been parsed for signs that the candidates are drawing supporters beyond their particular "minority" demographic. Over the past month and a half [January to mid-February 2008], the feminist pioneers Gloria Steinem and Robin Morgan have both published widely talked-about essays arguing that Clinton would have long since sewn up the nomination if not for the stubbornness of our national sexism. And when Clinton's primary victory in New Hampshire last month caught everyone by surprise, some analysts suggested that the polls had been so wrong beforehand in part because voters in the overwhelmingly white state had been reluctant to share their true, race-based reservations about Obama.

The discussion so far has been rather short on data. There have been surveys asking whether Americans would vote for a black or female candidate for President—according to a December 2007 Gallup poll, 93 percent and 86 percent, respectively, say they would. Those answers should be interpreted with some skepticism, however, because people are often unaware of their biases and don't tend to reveal them honestly in surveys.

But turn away from the campaign trail, and toward the laboratories where psychologists work, and a fascinating portrait of the primaries emerges. For decades, researchers have been probing bias—how it arises, how it changes, how it fades away. Their work suggests that bias plays a more powerful role in shaping opinions than most people are aware of. And they suggest that the American mind treats race and gender quite differently. Race can evoke more visceral, negative associations, the studies show, but attitudes toward women are more inflexible and—to judge by the current dynamics of the presidential race—ultimately more limiting.

"Gender stereotypes trump race stereotypes in every social science test," says Alice Eagly, a psychology professor at Northwestern University.

Research Points to Difficulties for Hillary Clinton

It would be a gross oversimplification to reduce the Democratic race to the white woman versus the black man. Factors like Obama's eloquence and inexperience and Clinton's policy mastery and her association with the ambivalent legacy of her husband have played a larger role in how the race has been talked about. And indeed, this presidential contest can be seen as the country's attempt to lurch beyond a blinkered, monolithic identity politics.

But in a campaign in which it's hard to find many substantive policy differences between the leading Democratic contenders, it's notable how well the psychological research on bias predicts

The Democratic primary contest between now-president Barack Obama and Hillary Clinton is viewed as the country's attempt to go beyond the identity politics of race and sex.

the race we've seen so far. Obama's ability to disarm the initial reservations of an increasing number of white voters as the race has progressed—especially over the past week [in February 2008], in his string of eight straight primary victories—fits with the findings of bias researchers that racial bias is strikingly mutable, and can be mitigated and even erased by everything from clothing and speech cadence to setting and skin tone.

As Clinton has discovered, gender stereotypes are stickier. Women can be seen as ambitious and capable, or they can be seen as likable, a host of studies have shown, but it's very hard for them to be seen as both—hence the intense scrutiny and much-debated impact of Clinton's moment of emotional vulnerability in a New Hampshire diner last month [January 2008].

As the race moves toward the possibly decisive March 4 [2008] primaries in Ohio and Texas, Clinton and Obama will have to continue to negotiate the complex demands of campaigning for an office that has been held by an unbroken string of 42 white men. But while this presidential campaign has proven a stage on which these issues can dramatically play out, they also run deeply through the rest of our society. And if the ample literature on bias shows anything, it is that, for all the difficulties Americans have with race, it may prove that attitudes about women are the hardest to change.

Race and gender are both traits that we cannot help but notice. One hundred milliseconds after we have first laid eyes on some-one, we have made a determination about their race; 50 millisec-onds later, we have determined their gender. But the reactions are not identical.

When psychologists talk about bias, they use three techni-cal categories: stereotyping, prejudice, and discrimination. Stereotyping is cognitive bias, the tendency to ascribe people a set of traits based on the group they belong to (e.g., "black people are good at sports," "Jews are cheap"). Prejudice is an emotional bias, disliking someone because of their group identity. And dis-crimination is how we act on the first two.

Sexual prejudice isn't terribly common—male chauvinists don't dislike women, they just have particular ideas about their capabilities and how they should behave—but with race, stereo-types tend to go hand-in-hand with prejudice.

Racial Prejudice Can Be Reduced

Many studies have shown the prevalence of negative asso-ciations among white Americans toward blacks. Mahzarin Banaji of Harvard and Anthony Greenwald of the University of Washington have done influential work showing that most whites, whatever their professed racial attitudes, are quicker to associate positive words with images of whites, and quicker to associate negative words with blacks. The test they developed, the Implicit Association Test, or IAT, has become one of the most common tools for measuring bias.

Joshua Correll, a psychology professor at the University of Chicago, measures bias in a more dynamic way, looking at associations with danger. In one set of studies he had mostly white participants play a primitive video game in which they had to make split-second "shoot/no-shoot" decisions based on whether the figure on the screen was holding a gun. Most subjects, he found, were more trigger-happy when presented with an image of a black man.

But follow-up studies have also shown that these biases can be sharply reduced, and in some cases even erased. When participants, for example, are shown images of well-liked black public figures before taking the IAT, their anti-black biases disappear.

"We're finding that racial stereotyping and prejudice are extremely contextual," says Correll. "You can see real reductions in prejudice, and sometimes it actually reverses," crossing over into a sort of stereotypic affinity.

And this, Correll argues, works to the advantage of someone like Obama. "You look at Obama, and he represents himself incredibly well," Correll says. "There are a whole lot of contextual cues that tell us this is someone you don't need to worry about."

The pollster John Zogby sees some signs that white voters have grown more comfortable with black candidates. He offers the example of Harold Ford, the young, black Democratic congressman who narrowly lost his bid for one of Tennessee's US Senate seats in 2006. Traditionally, Zogby points out, black candidates do worse on Election Day than in pre-election polling because people tell pollsters they're more comfortable with black candidates than they actually are—this phenomenon, the so-called Bradley Effect, is what some analysts thought helped Clinton . . . in New Hampshire. But, Zogby points out, Ford actually did better in the final vote than in pre-election polling, suggesting a dissipation of the Bradley Effect.

Some of the most dramatic work in racial bias mitigation was published in 2001 by John Tooby and Leda Cosmides, a husband-and-wife team of evolutionary psychologists at the University of California, Santa Barbara, and their then-student Robert Kurzban. In their study, they presented participants with a series of images of people, each with a sentence that the person in the image had supposedly said. Later on, the test subject would be asked to recall who had said what.

What they were after were wrong answers. The ways in which test subjects misattributed quotes betrayed the categories by which they grouped people. Subjects, for example, were far more apt to misattribute something one black man had said to another black man, rather than to a white man or to a woman.

Surprisingly, though, the researchers found that they were able to get people to stop paying attention to race with a simple manipulation: they showed images of people wearing one of two colors of T-shirts, paired with quotes that gave the impression that the T-shirts correlated with membership on different "teams." In response, test-takers started grouping people on the basis of the T-shirt color rather than their skin color, confusing T-shirt "team members" of different ethnicities with each other.

And while the study wasn't looking at bias, the implications are clear. "If you're going to discriminate on the basis of race you first have to notice it," says Kurzban, now at the University of Pennsylvania. In an experimental setting, at least, he argues, you can get people to stop doing that.

The researchers didn't see a similar effect for gender. According to Tooby, "People can cease to notice ethnicity as a factor in how they conceptualize somebody in a way that they don't seem to be able to with gender."

Gender Stereotyping Tends to Be Strong

There is work suggesting that implicit gender stereotypes can also display a degree of mutability, at least among women. Studies conducted by Nilanjana Dasgupta, a psychology professor at the University of Massachusetts, Amherst, have found that exposing women to photos and biographical information about accomplished women like Meg Whitman, CEO [chief executive officer] of eBay, or the Supreme Court justice Ruth Bader Ginsburg did undermine the stereotypes the women taking the test held about the incompatibility of women and leadership.

Still, psychologists specializing in gender bias say that many studies have shown how strong a force gender stereotyping is. In one particularly telling strain of research, called the Goldberg paradigm, two sets of participants are asked to comment on something, perhaps a resume or a speech or a work scenario in which a boss speaks with an employee. To one audience, the person involved is described as a woman, in the other he is a man. Time and again, male participants (and, in some cases, women as well) judge the resume more harshly if it is a woman's, or say the speech was strident if given by a woman but assertive if given by a man, or that the female boss was pushy while the male boss was concerned.

Women in these studies are typically judged to be less capable than men with identical qualifications, but it's not impossible for them to be seen as competent. The problem is that if they're understood to be capable, the majority or respondents also see them as less likable. "The deal is that women generally fall into two alternatives: they are either seen as nice but stupid or smart but mean," says Susan Fiske, a psychology professor at Princeton who specializes in stereotyping.

And unlike racial bias, there's little evidence that these attitudes are softening. According to Eagly of Northwestern, the problem isn't that women aren't traditionally understood as smart, but that they traditionally aren't understood to be "assertive, competitive, take-charge" types. More than intelligence, she argues, this "agentic" quality is what we look for in leaders, and, as both surveys and experimental studies have shown, we find it deeply discomfiting in women. "That's what Hillary Clinton is up against," argues Eagly. "She's had to show her toughness, then people turn around and say she's too cold."

Amy Cuddy, a psychologist at Northwestern, suggests that the durability of gender stereotypes stems in part from the fact that

Majority of Americans Would Vote for a Minority Presidential Candidate

Women still struggle to be elected to the highest office in the United States. Many Americans seem ready at least to consider a wide variety of minority candidates, but women candidates are at the bottom of the list.

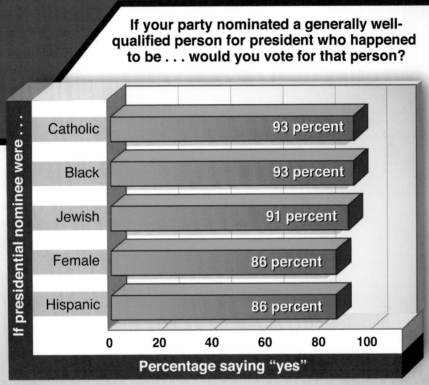

If your party nominated a generally well-qualified person for president who happened to be . . . would you vote for that person?

If presidential nominee were . . .

	Percentage saying "yes"
Catholic	93 percent
Black	93 percent
Jewish	91 percent
Female	86 percent
Hispanic	86 percent

Taken from: 2007 Gallup poll, "Race: People's Chief Concerns," www.publicagenda.org.

most people have far more exposure to people of the opposite gender than to people of different races. As a result, they feel more entitled to their attitudes about gender. "Contact hasn't undermined these stereotypes, and it might even strengthen them," she says. "Many people don't believe seeing women as kind or soft is a stereotype. They're not even going to question it, because they think it's a good thing."

Tooby takes a more biological view. As he argues, in the pre-historic environment in which our brains evolved, race had no meaning—no one could travel far enough to meet anyone who didn't look like them. Gender, on the other hand, meant a lot. It predicted what someone's status would be, what their priorities were, whether they were a potential rival or a potential partner.

Indeed, the only other trait that we notice as strongly as gender, Tooby points out, is age. Clinton is 60 years old, Obama 46. And no matter who wins the Democratic nomination, the face-off against the 71-year-old John McCain may introduce a whole new aspect to the identity politics of the campaign.

SIX

Ban on Gay Marriage Is Prejudice

Kenji Yoshino

> Kenji Yoshino is an author and professor at Yale Law School. In the following editorial originally published in *The New York Times*, Yoshino summarizes court rulings upholding state bans on same-sex marriages. Yoshino examines the courts' arguments and asserts that the judges are stereotyping gay relationships and discriminating against gays.

In 2006 New York's highest court voted 4-to-2 that a legislative ban on same-sex marriage did not violate the state Constitution. In doing so, it added to the patchwork of state rulings on the issue, including those of Indiana and Arizona (which similarly upheld legislative bans) and Massachusetts (which struck down a legislative ban).

What's noteworthy about the New York decision, however, is that it became the second ruling by a state high court to assert a startling rationale for prohibiting same-sex marriage—that straight couples may be less stable parents than their gay counterparts and consequently require the benefits of marriage to assist them.

The critical question, expressed in a plurality opinion by three members of the New York court, is whether a "rational legislature" could decide that the benefits of marriage should be granted to

Kenji Yoshino, "Too Good for Marriage," *New York Times*, July 14, 2006. Reprinted with permission.

41

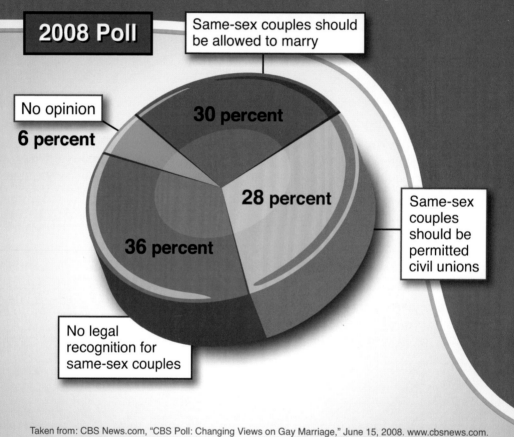

American Views on Gay Marriage Are Changing

Although gays still struggle for equal rights in marriage and partnerships, a recent poll shows that the number of Americans who support same-sex marriage is increasing. In 2004 the same poll showed that just 21 percent of Americans were in support of same-sex marriage.

2008 Poll

Same-sex couples should be allowed to marry

No opinion

6 percent

30 percent

28 percent

36 percent

Same-sex couples should be permitted civil unions

No legal recognition for same-sex couples

Taken from: CBS News.com, "CBS Poll: Changing Views on Gay Marriage," June 15, 2008. www.cbsnews.com.

opposite-sex couples but not to same-sex couples. The opinion then answered in the affirmative with two different arguments. While both related to the interests of children, they differed significantly in vintage and tone.

The more traditional argument stated that the Legislature could reasonably suppose that children would fare better under the care of a mother and father. Like most arguments against gay marriage, this "role model" argument assumes straight couples are better guides to life than gay couples.

And like other blatantly anti-gay arguments, it falls apart under examination. In a decision last month [June 2006] in a case concerning gay foster parents, the Arkansas Supreme Court found no evidence that children raised by gay couples were disadvantaged compared with children raised by straight couples.

But the New York court also put forth another argument, sometimes called the "reckless procreation" rationale. "Heterosexual intercourse," the plurality opinion stated, "has a natural tendency to lead to the birth of children; homosexual intercourse does not." Gays become parents, the opinion said, in a variety of ways, including adoption and artificial insemination, "but they do not become parents as a result of accident or impulse." Consequently, "the Legislature could find that unstable relationships between people of the opposite sex present a greater danger that children will be born into or grow up in unstable homes than is the case with same-sex couples."

To shore up those rickety heterosexual arrangements, "the Legislature could rationally offer the benefits of marriage to opposite-sex couples only." Lest we miss the inversion of stereotypes about gay relationships here, the opinion lamented that straight relationships are "all too often casual or temporary."

When an Indiana court introduced this seemingly heterophobic logic last year [2005] in upholding a state ban on same-sex marriage, I thought it was a cockeyed aberration. But after both New York City and New York State presented similar logic in oral arguments, and the court followed suit, I began to understand the argument's appeal: it sounds nicer to gays.

It also sounds more desperate. New York's ban on same-sex marriage is based on provisions enacted in 1909. It is preposterous to suggest the Legislature promulgated and retained the law because it believed gays to be better parents. Moreover, as New York's chief judge, Judith Kaye, pointed out in her dissent, even if marriage were a response to the dangers of "reckless procreation," excluding gay couples from marriage in no way advances the goal of responsible heterosexual child-rearing. "There are enough marriage licenses to go around for everyone," Judge Kaye noted.

This is not the first time courts have restricted rights with a flourish of fond regards. In 1873, the United States Supreme Court upheld an Illinois statute prohibiting women from practicing law. Concurring in that judgment, Justice Joseph Bradley observed that the "natural and proper timidity and delicacy" of women better suited them to "the noble and benign offices of wife and mother."

Hostile rulings delivered in friendly tones can take longer to overturn, as evidenced by the century that passed before members

Some people say that New York's ban on gay marriage is based on provisions enacted in a law in 1909, which are not relevant to today's society.

OBTAIN

MARRIAGE

LICENSES

HERE

of the Supreme Court reversed their thinking about women and, in a 1973 opinion in a sex discrimination case, recognized that confining women in the name of cherishing them put them "not on a pedestal, but in a cage."

We should not need a century to unmask the "reckless procreation" argument as a new guise for an old prejudice. The "reckless procreation" argument sounds nicer—and may even be nicer—than the plainly derogatory "role model" argument. But equality would be nicer still.

SEVEN

Opposition to Gay Marriage Is Not Prejudice

Aryeh Spero

Aryeh Spero is a rabbi, radio talk-show host, and president of Caucus for America, a conservative political organization. In the following article he argues that laws making same-sex marriages illegal are not due to prejudice. Instead, he asserts that they are about preserving the long-held tradition of marriage between a man and a woman. Spero makes the case that since gays can marry if they want to marry someone of the opposite sex, no real discrimination is taking place.

The claim made by advocates of gay marriage and its proponents such as the *New York Times* and Senator Teddy Kennedy is that a ban of gay marriage is simply about prejudice and bigotry. They are wrong. It is simply about the definition of marriage, regardless of sexual habit.

Furthermore, discrimination rooted in prejudice means we do not allow a person of a particular race, religion or sexual orientation to participate in our existing institutions or enjoy the same activities others do. But no one in America would deny an avowed gay man to get married, like all other men, to a woman. Marriage of gays is not problematic, rather same-sex marriage.

Aryeh Spero, "Opposition to Gay Marriage Is Not Discrimination," Human Events.com, June 8, 2006. Reproduced by permission.

Gays Can Marry

Nor is the law prejudiced against any proclaimed lesbian wishing, like other women, to marry a man. Who they are does not enter the equation. Whatever their announced orientation, gays have the same right as everyone else to marriage as defined, across the board, by our laws and history: the union of one man (whatever his sexual orientation) to one woman (whatever her orientation). The existing institution of marriage is open to all.

Marriage is a contract, and as with all contracts there are elements that define it and superimpose on those committing to it. For the contract to be legal and binding, each party to it must abide by its inherent elements. In this case, the elements are one man, one woman.

Supporters of banning same-sex marriage say that their concerns are about preserving the sanctity of marriage and not about prejudices toward gays and lesbians.

The problem lies not in the "wannabes" because of who they are, but rather because what they want to do does not exist for anybody. Green is not red; and the rules of football do not extend to baseball simply because it is also a sport.

In times past when blacks were denied the right to vote, it was discrimination since others had that right. When in certain

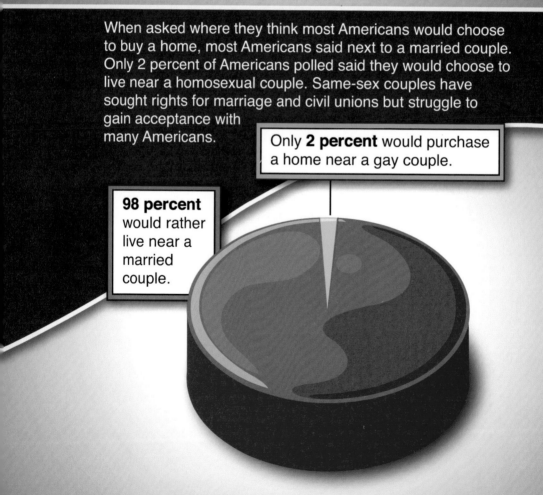

The Vast Majority of Americans Would Rather Live Near a Married Couple

When asked where they think most Americans would choose to buy a home, most Americans said next to a married couple. Only 2 percent of Americans polled said they would choose to live near a homosexual couple. Same-sex couples have sought rights for marriage and civil unions but struggle to gain acceptance with many Americans.

Only **2 percent** would purchase a home near a gay couple.

98 percent would rather live near a married couple.

Taken from: Philip A. Vauno, *American Prejudice*, Logby International, July 2007.

locales in deep medieval Europe Jews were forbidden to marry it was discrimination since all others could marry. These were discriminations and exclusions born of prejudice based not on what but who. Once given the right to marry, it would have been preposterous for a Jew to claim discrimination if the state outlawed him from marrying, for example, an aunt. Nor could a black man cry discrimination if after being given the right to vote he demanded that he be allowed to vote while underage.

The *New York Times* sermonizes that denying gays marriage deprives them of equal protection. That argument is erroneous, for when we allow people of differing religion, race, gender or sexual orientation to participate and share in categories defined equally for all, discrimination does not exist.

Preserving Integrity of Marriage Is Important

Certainly prejudice against gays is not at the root of those wishing to preserve the integrity of marriage. Those opposed to same-sex marriage do not advocate against gays the historic discriminations— such as denial of voting, housing, employment, etc.

That the issue revolves around a definition and not the people involved is clear when considering the following scenario: what if two straight guys decided to get married for the singular purpose of bypassing all sorts of business legalities and "lawyering" in order to create community property from their combined two businesses. Though they are not gay, the law would still deny them a license to marry, since the union of two men does not fall within the definition of marriage, even where homosexuality is not involved. It is not the homosexuality per se but the union of the same-gendered that is oxymoronic with marriage.

All things are not the same. However, through the unanswered assertions of moral relativism, all things are deemed the same, and thus meaningless. The problem bedeviling society over the last 40 years is more than having been asked to tolerate and accept modes of conduct heretofore outside the respectable pale. It is that those engaged in those activities demand that society redefine its institutions and overturn cherished and wise traditions in order not only to accommodate but also affirm as equally legitimate and desirable such activities.

Special Privileges for Gays Is Not the Answer

Most often, they are accorded special privileges, with the government zealously targeting employers to meet quotas and, first, prove their innocence in hiring and rental practices if they are to be free from penalization. What begins as a person's or group's desire for private, individual expression always ends up with that activity being given public sanctification, with regular citizens bearing the financial costs.

These redefinitions result in the banalization and degradation of the previously accepted standards and practices. Worse, language is reconfigured so that, for example, husbands are simply partners, wives are simply spouses. Sex education will be forced to teach about the alternatively valid same-sex marriage, and woe to those parents and students who balk: the power of the government will come down upon them harshly.

Will churches and synagogues that cite Scripture forbidding such marriage be indicted for hate speech? They will be! We hear about gay rights, never first realizing that what ultimately will be taken from most everyone else will be freedom of speech and religion; our privacy itself. Our tolerance for the unconventional will result in federal intolerance for the conventional, the necessary.

The upshot, as we have seen with other causes, is the diminution, marginalization and even disempowerment of those too mainstream to be counted among the exotic or preferentialed minorities. Quite often that is precisely the underlying, ulterior motive of the iconoclast and gatecrasher.

EIGHT

Prejudice Can Be Understood and Reduced

Graham Wagstaff

> Graham Wagstaff is a professor of psychology at the University of Liverpool, where he has taught primarily social and forensic psychology since 1973. He has published extensively on a variety of topics, including the social psychology of justice and eyewitness testimony. In the following viewpoint Wagstaff defines prejudice and explains different theories about what causes discrimination and prejudice, describing both cultural and cognitive theories on why people are prejudiced. He contends that understanding prejudice can help us reduce it. Wagstaff concludes by offering suggestions for ways we can reduce prejudice and discrimination. He argues that both education and legislation are important.

Social psychologists typically define prejudice as an unjustified negative attitude towards a group or its members. Prejudice is manifested in a distortion of perception, and occurs in three main ways.

- First, information is selectively admitted or rejected. For example, to a male chauvinist, if statistics show that women take more time off work than men, the statistics are welcomed

Graham Wagstaff, "Understanding Prejudice," *Psychology Review*, vol. 11, April 2005, pp. 20–23. Reproduced by permission.

as valid, but if they show that women generally get more work than men, they are rejected.

- Second, similar information is differently interpreted to fit the prejudice. So, if a white racist sees a white person driving a very expensive car, he may think that the driver is a successful entrepreneur. However, if the driver is black, the racist is more likely to think that the driver is a drugs dealer or has stolen the car.
- Third, contradictory information is interpreted to fit the prejudice. For example, research has shown that people who are anti-Semitic often accuse Jews of being both overly intrusive (prying into others' affairs) and overly seclusive (keeping themselves to themselves).

Whereas prejudice reflects essentially how we feel about or evaluate others, discrimination concerns overt acts of acceptance or rejection of a person or group. Hence, people who show discrimination may not necessarily be prejudiced. For example, in the past, New York taxi cab drivers, many of whom were black, would sometimes refuse to pick up black passengers, not because the drivers were prejudiced, but because the cab companies had told the drivers that they would lose their jobs if they carried black people. Nevertheless, most researchers believe that discrimination against a person or group is usually the behavioural expression of prejudice somewhere down the line.

So what are the causes of prejudice and discrimination? Theories of prejudice and discrimination have been categorised in numerous ways, but one useful categorisation is described here.

Causes of Prejudice

According to the cultural approach, prejudice reflects prevailing cultural norms. For example, economic exploitation theory argues that prejudice is an attitude or set of norms, propagated by a ruling class for the purpose of stigmatising a group as inferior (O.C. Cox 1948). A good historical example concerns the emergence of prejudiced beliefs in the eighteenth and nineteenth centuries to justify slavery. If certain racial groups are considered to be little better than animals, then it is easier to justify using them as slave labour.

However, this theory does not consider individual differences. Why, within an exploiting class, should some individuals be more prejudiced than others? Also, it cannot account easily for prejudice against those who are not obviously the objects of economic exploitation, such as gay people and Quakers. Perhaps most important, a variety of evidence suggests that, in terms of social class groupings, most prejudice appears in groups who might be considered exploited—those of low social and economic status.

An alternative view is that prejudice results from conflict. According to realistic conflict theory, prejudice arises when people are placed in actual conflict with others. The conflict can arise from

According to conflict theory, prejudices arise when people are placed in conflict with others as they compete for jobs, money, and status.

competition for a variety of resources, including territory, money, jobs and status. Probably the most famous studies used to support this view are [Muzater] Sherif's (1966) studies of young boys in summer camp. Sherif and his colleagues found that prejudice and discrimination increased when the boys were separated into groups and made to compete for goals. More recent research indicates that prejudice against immigrants in the USA and Switzerland is highly related to whether people consider immigrants to be a threat to their economic well-being. But again, this theory does not account for individual differences within groups, and prejudice against groups not associated with competition for resources (such as gays). Neither does it tell us the mechanism whereby conflict translates to prejudice.

Perhaps the least satisfactory cultural approach to prejudice and discrimination is the earned reputation theory. This suggests that prejudice norms arise from 'kernels of truth'. But if the negative stereotypes that people adopt about different racial groups are based on truth, they are not entirely unjustified and cannot be considered prejudiced. And if the argument is that the kernels of truth are elaborated to give rise to prejudice, how does this happen? The theory does not tell us.

The Motivational Approach

Others have directed their attention away from the situation to look at the motivation of the individual. Frustration–aggression (scapegoat) theory argues that prejudice is an outlet for frustration and aggression. According to this theory, when frustrated, people may displace their resulting aggression onto a powerless and often irrelevant group. A famous study that is often linked to frustration–aggression theory is one that examined the relationship between the number of lynchings for a given year in the southern states of the USA, between 1882 and 1930. The researchers found that they could predict the number of lynchings from a knowledge of the price of cotton for that year. As the price of cotton dropped (and presumably people became worried and frustrated), the number of lynchings increased (C.I. Hovland and R.R. Sears 1940).

However, again, the theory does not explain the mechanism whereby frustration and aggression translate into prejudice. Moreover, people can develop prejudice without necessarily being frustrated. For example, if individuals are randomly assigned to groups (creating what are known as 'minimal groups'), they may develop unjustified negative attitudes towards those in other groups ('out-groups').

The Cognitive Approach

To cope with these difficulties, other theorists have adopted a more cognitive approach and suggest that prejudice is almost a natural consequence of the way we process information. For example, social identity theory (L.H. Tajfel 1982) proposes a three-stage process.

- First, through normal cognitive processes, people categorise others into groups or classes.
- Second, they strive to maintain a positive self-concept by identifying with a group.
- Third, they promote their own groups so that they will appear better than other groups.

As a consequence, to enhance their own status, people tend to over-reward their own in-group, and denigrate out-groups. In accordance with the work on minimal groups, this theory predicts that people will show allegiance to groups based on random and superficial characteristics. Another prediction from the theory is that prejudice will be greatest among those whose self-concept has been threatened. In support of this, J.R. Meindl and M.J. Lerner (1985) found that French- and English-speaking Canadians made more negative statements about each other when they had an accident that made them feel embarrassed.

Self-categorisation theory was derived from social identity theory and explores in more detail the processes by which categorisation occurs. The idea is that we tend to stereotype not only out-groups but our own in-groups. These stereotypes, or prototypes, tend both to minimise in-group differences and to exaggerate inter-group differences. Related to this, recent research suggests that people stereotypically attribute more human emotions to their own in-groups and consider out-groups as less human. This results in less empathy for the out-group and makes it easier to discriminate against them.

Although cognitive in orientation, both social identity and self-categorisation theories maintain a motivational component, in that people are assumed to receive some emotional benefit from identifying with a particular group. Another version of the cognitive approach, however, argues that prejudice can occur simply through mistakes in the way we process information. According to social cognition theory, prejudice arises because people use judgmental heuristics or short cuts when judging others. For example, we tend to group things together simply because they bear a superficial resemblance and/or are distinctive in some way.

In Western culture, real life negative events are distinctive because they are less common than neutral or positive events (for instance, most of us are not robbed on a daily basis). Also, to the majority, minority groups are more distinctive because the majority have less contact with them. As a consequence, through a process known as illusory correlation, negative attributes are often associated with minority groups.

However, again, cognitive theories have little to say about individual differences in prejudice. One could argue, perhaps, on the basis of social identity theory, that variations in the strength of self-concepts might give rise to variation within groups, but still, individual differences do not form a core feature of the cognitive approach. In contrast, other theories have concentrated more closely on the role of individual differences.

Personality and Individual Differences in Prejudice

Authoritarian personality theory (T.W. Adorno et al. 1950) is based primarily on psychoanalytic principles, and proposes that prejudice is most likely to arise in families that try to enforce conventional values through harsh discipline. According to the theory, because of guilt and fear of punishment, children reared in such environments cannot direct their resulting frustration and aggression towards the legitimate target—their parents—so they displace these feelings onto other groups in the form of prejudice and discrimination. Along with this, a number of other characteristics develop which, collectively, make up nine components of the authoritarian personality—that is, the type of person who is most likely to be prejudiced. These components are: conventionalism, authoritarian submission, authoritarian aggression, anti-intraception (dislike of emotional sensitivity), superstition and stereotypy, power and toughness, destructiveness, projectivity (attributing unacceptable impulses to others) and preoccupation with sex. To measure these characteristics, the researchers developed a questionnaire known as the F-scale, which has been used widely as a research tool.

The F-scale has received considerable criticism, mainly because it might reflect educational status rather than personality. Other studies, however, have found considerable support for the F-scale and the hypothesised relationship between authoritarianism and prejudice. For example, recent studies show a relationship between F-scores and prejudice against AIDS sufferers and the homeless. Moreover, research from Canada shows that dominating authoritarians remain among the most prejudiced people in society today. Significantly, it also seems that authoritarianism may vary over time; F-scores increase in times of economic threat, and particularly in response to out-group threat. This suggests a possible overlap between the authoritarian personality approach and the realistic conflict and frustration-aggression approaches to prejudice and discrimination.

Another approach to individual differences in prejudice also relates prejudice to the experience of threat. According to the just world theory, we have a fundamental need to believe that justice exists in the world (Z. Rubin and L.A. Peplau 1975). Hence, when we see people suffering by chance, our belief in a just world is threatened. One way of restoring this belief is to adopt unjustified negative attitudes to those who are victims of suffering (so it appears that they deserve to suffer). And, as some people need to believe in a just world more than others, this accounts for individual differences in prejudice.

In support of this theory, a variety of research, both archival and experimental, supports the view that victims of misfortune (such as victims of rape and assault) are often derogated in an attempt to make out that they deserve what happens to them. One can perhaps see an overlap here with the economic exploitation explanation—exploiters may attempt to maintain their belief in a just world by derogating those they exploit.

However, although the authoritarian personality and just world theories seem to have some merit, not all those who are prejudiced are authoritarian or believe in a just world. For example, research on racist groups in Britain suggests that although authoritarians are well represented, others do not display authoritarian characteristics. Some individuals seem to use prejudice and discrimination merely as outlets for their aggressive tendencies. But again, some familiar themes seem to emerge.

Integrating the Approaches of Prejudice and Discrimination

Although it may be tempting at first to conclude that psychologists simply cannot agree on the causes of prejudice, the emergence of some common themes suggests that it may be possible to integrate the approaches into an overall picture. One such integrating scheme is presented below. The basic idea is to divide the components of the various theories into six progressive levels.

1. Situation. Two overriding themes underlying most of these theories are the notions of conflict and threat arising from the situations in which people find themselves or in which they have been placed. These can arise from general social causes (economic conflict, war, poverty) or personal causes (harsh upbringing, rejection, loss).
2. Affect. These sources of conflict and threat may give rise to a variety of affective responses, including feelings of anxiety, frustration, aggression and lack of self-esteem.
3. Cognition. When we experience these affective responses, we are more likely to employ cognitive devices such as social categorisation, judgmental heuristics, projection and creating scapegoats.

4. Attitudes and behaviour. As a result of these cognitive processes, we are more likely to form unjustified negative attitudes towards others and discriminate against out-groups/scapegoats.
5. Rationalisation. If our attitudes and behaviours are unjustified, they may cause internal and external conflict, so we may engage in various forms of rationalisation to maintain cognitive consistency and our belief in a just world.
6. Persistence and elaboration. The rationalisation results in the persistence and elaboration of prejudice and discrimination. These produce yet more conflict and the cycle is perpetuated.

Americans Are Optimistic About Race Relations

Educators and activists assert that prejudice can be reduced, and polls show that Americans are beginning to feel optimistic about race relations in the United States.

In a 2007 Gallup poll, people were asked: *"Do you think that race relations between blacks and whites will always be a problem for the United States or that a solution will eventually be worked out?"*

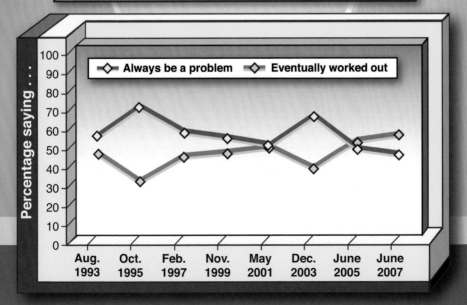

Taken from: 2007 Gallup poll, "Race: People's Chief Concerns." www.publicagenda.org.

Reducing Prejudice

All this has implications for how we might reduce prejudice. According to the above scheme, there are a number of points at which we can intervene. Obviously it is difficult, though not always impossible, to intervene at the level of basic conflict (by creating economic stability or reducing poverty). However, there are other things that can be done. For example, one approach is to provide detailed and accurate information to counter the inaccurate beliefs that occur as a result of processes such as social categorisation, judgmental heuristics and rationalisation. Actual contact with out-groups is particularly useful in this respect, as this can counter inaccurate beliefs and also promote empathy and reduce anxiety. Nevertheless, research also suggests that simple contact alone is not sufficient; rather, along with contact, there must be close interaction, the atmosphere must be cooperative and positive and the groups must be of equal status.

Ultimately, perhaps the most important elements for reducing prejudice are education and legislation. Although there are obvious exceptions, we know that, in general, the more educated people are, the less they are likely to be prejudiced. There are a number of reasons for this. As well as providing necessary information to counter inaccurate beliefs, education promotes reflection and critical analysis and reduces the likelihood of people making simple heuristic judgments. Legislation is important because, as research on attitudes and behaviour informs us, one of the most effective ways of changing attitudes is to change behaviour. If we legislate against prejudice and discrimination, people will have to rationalise their conduct to fall in line with the law. So, ironically, just as justification and rationalisation often lead to prejudice and discrimination, they can also be used as valuable tools to combat these problems.

Notes

T.W. Adorno et al., *The Authoritarian Personality*. New York: Harper and Row, 1950.

O.C. Cox, *Caste, Class and Race*. New York: Doubleday, 1948.

C.I. Hovland and R.R. Sears, 'Minor Studies in Aggression: VI. Correlation of Lynchings with Economic Indices,' *Journal of Psychology*, 1940, vol. 9, pp. 301–10.

J.R. Meindl and M.J. Lerner, 'Exacerbation of Extreme Responses to an Outgroup,' *Journal of Personality and Social Psychology*, 1985, vol. 47, pp. 71–84.

Z. Rubin and L.A. Peplau, 'Who Believes in a Just World?' *Journal of Social Issues*, 1975, vol. 3, pp. 65–89.

M. Sherif, *In Common Predicament: Social Psychology of Inter-group Conflict and Cooperation*. Boston: Houghton Mifflin, 1966.

H. Tajfel, *Social Identity and Intergroup Relations*. Cambridge, UK: Cambridge University Press, 1982.

NINE

Diversity Curriculum Can Help Reduce Prejudice

Judith Gaston Fisher

Judith Gaston Fisher is a teaching specialist at Community School in Missouri. In this article she discusses the importance of teaching diversity to both students and educators. Her students were willing, able, and even eager to discuss differences related to race and culture. Fisher emphasizes the importance of open communication in the classroom, as well as the benefits of using a variety of materials related to the topic of diversity.

For some 20 years, while working at various independent schools, I have observed a new, but undefined, curriculum emerging—one that has centered on educating children to tolerate, accept, appreciate, and learn from others different from themselves. We file these initiatives under the catch-all category of diversity and recognize both the need and the desirability of building institutions and communities in which different backgrounds, races, and cultures are fully represented and valued. But I've also observed that, at many of these schools, such initiatives have not been as successful as their creators intended. Often, they have been trial-and-error endeavors whose outcomes were not measured and whose results, therefore, were uncertain. All this is not due to a lack

Judith Gaston Fisher, "Let's Talk About It!" *Independent School,* vol. 67, Fall 2007, pp. 14–17. Reproduced by permission.

of commitment, nor is it a question of believing in the importance of diversity work, nor is it from an absence of academic study and research. As I see it, the problem in teaching our children to develop positive attitudes toward culture, race, and ethnicity has not been in the "what" or the "why," but largely in the "how." How exactly do we help students navigate the inclusive classroom and community?

Call it multicultural education, diversity, or cultural sensitivity training, each initiative I've been involved with has comprised important concepts of race, culture, religion, and socioeconomic status. But where was a school to start in developing an elementary child's sensitivity and understanding regarding these topics?

What Should Diversity Education Look Like?

Often the process of program development began with round-table discussions among administrators in which questions predominated. Should teachers be educated first? What about parents? Should we mail informational fliers to them? Should teachers conduct curriculum nights? Should parents be required to attend school-supported race and equity workshops? And what about the children? Were there any "best practices" we could adopt? Should it be a separate curriculum or integrated into academic subject areas or the character education program?

At Community School (Missouri), where I work, educating the faculty of pre-kindergarten-through-sixth-grade students became the first line of attack. Seminars and in-service training focused on identifying, addressing, and role-playing stereotypes. The entire staff watched movies (e.g., *Brown Eyes, Blue Eyes*) and read books (e.g., *Race Manners*) and discussed their meaning and application to our community. Teachers attended multicultural conferences and summer workshops. And various committees were formed—the committee on holidays and celebrations; one uniting the board, teachers, and parents; and one for designing international potlucks and gatherings.

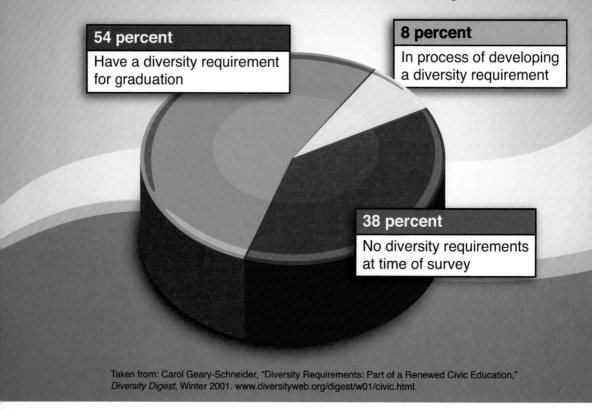

Diversity Requirements in American Colleges

A survey of 543 American colleges shows that most colleges require some kind of diversity course as a requirement to graduate with a bachelor's degree.

54 percent

Have a diversity requirement for graduation

8 percent

In process of developing a diversity requirement

38 percent

No diversity requirements at time of survey

Taken from: Carol Geary-Schneider, "Diversity Requirements: Part of a Renewed Civic Education," *Diversity Digest*, Winter 2001. www.diversityweb.org/digest/w01/civic.html.

Translating Diversity Education into Real Interactions

Even so, it was still not clear how all this translated into the daily interactions between teacher and students.

Last September [2006], I found myself leaving the world of administration to re-enter the classroom. Classified as a learning specialist, I now sought to squarely face the issues I had addressed in a more indirect fashion, usually from the safe remove of a committee member engaged in interminable planning sessions. I was now alone with students, in my own classroom behind closed doors, facing the necessity of developing a realistic approach to a persistent challenge. How would I apply the tools and techniques of education to increase appreciation of cultural and racial diversity and to address the powerful cluster of harmful attitudes and practices we commonly associate with stereotyping and racism?

It was time, I believed, to roll up my sleeves and jump in feet first, to practice what I preached. I sought to go beyond class meetings and literature studies where issues were caged in the safety of fictional characters. Instead, I desired to hit these issues head-on, using reliable data and real-life stories as a vehicle for discussion. I admit to second thoughts when I thought about engaging students in sensitive racial discussions. I feared parent and administrative reaction. I feared perceiving the influence of stereotypes where none existed. I feared my lack of expertise. But a persistent and honest desire to raise awareness drove me forward, a desire to uncover the veil of fear surrounding the issue of race.

A small group of sixth graders became my target group. My initial materials: stories from current newspapers and journals, as well as the perspectives presented in Bruce Jacobs' *Race Manners*, a book previously studied and discussed by the faculty. We blended literature and social studies material: Paul Fleischman's *Seedfolks*, Lois Lowry's *The Giver*, and Mildred Taylor's *The Land* complemented the students' study of the Civil War and ancient cultures. The material gave psychological depth and emotional resonance to issues that provide an important key to understanding the foundations of societies and the conflicts that can wrench them apart. I often asked students to extrapolate to the current state of racial affairs in the United States. A connection could be made from the past to the present to the future. It was a beginning.

That first day when I sat down with my class—not exactly a cross-section of America, but diverse in its own distinctive way (i.e., white, African American, Jewish, and Christian)—I was scared. I had sought advice from several teachers, had spent considerable time planning my introduction, and had chosen the particular themes I wanted to discuss. Still, I was hesitant.

Attempting to be confident and to project an air of assurance, I began by having the students design guidelines for these "important discussions." We defined respect, honesty, and confidentiality. We even implemented a sort of fail-safe measure. Anyone could invoke the "ouch" rule—that is, just say "ouch" whenever anyone uses a word or broached a topic that made others fearful or have hurt feelings.

Starting a Conversation on Stereotypes and Prejudice

And then I threw out the question: "If you were getting on a bus by yourself and the only open seats were next to a black man wearing baggy, low slung jeans, a Hispanic, or an Asian, what seat would you choose?"

There was dead silence, eyes darting sideways, heads down trying to hide in the pages of a notebook. "What is the first thought that jumped into your head?" I asked, my gaze moving from one individual to another. Finally, a hand shot up. "Well, I have a Mexican gardener so I am comfortable around Hispanics." That comment seemed to open the door for further exploration.

"I am really afraid of anyone speaking another language," offered a quiet, rather reticent young man. "It makes me nervous."

"I think it's the baggy pants that bothers me. When I'm in the mall, seeing someone dressed like that makes me uncomfortable. But I remember last year there was a black—I mean, an African American—sixth grader here who wore baggy pants and a large earring. His pants were always neat and clean. And boy, was he ever a good football player," commented another.

"What race usually dresses like that?" I asked.

"Blacks, or African Americans. What term should we use anyway?" questioned the boy who had spoken about the baggy pants. "I never know what is correct so I just don't use anything!"

And so the conversation that ensued attempted to explore and discuss racial terminology, stereotypes and racism, accepted preconceptions, and "you have a problem" indicators. As the students left that first day, I felt a mixture of success and pride as I looked forward to what our next day together might bring.

As part of diversity education, students are asked to discuss their views on prejudice.

Weeks later, I had become accustomed to hearing, "Hey, Mrs. Fisher, is this a 'Talk Day'? All right!"—a frequent question tossed out as these sixth graders entered the door. Talk Day was a term coined by the students to indicate class time devoted to the exploration of these issues of race and identity. Topics of discussion were as varied as my students. We learned about identifying real fear and fear that bubbles up just because of skin color or dress. We studied statistics regarding the separation and differential treatment of minorities in our own community. Who was more likely to get pulled over by traffic police? We talked about affirmative action and the apparent re-segregation of our public schools. Topics from the news media had a way of making it onto our conversational agenda: charges against three members of the Duke lacrosse team and reports of genocide in the Darfur region of Sudan.

Students Apply What They Learn

While I believed that my students were beginning to understand past and present day stereotypes, I needed more than just excitement to confirm that Talk Day was making a difference. I began to watch and note the students' mannerisms: Rachel,[1] herself Jewish, was confident and verbal and ready to argue a wide range of issues; Hunter, who was white, was a sensitive boy whose head often remained resting on an arm as he saved his stories and comments until the end of class; Yolanda, the lone black girl, whose eyes gave not a glimpse of anger, acceptance, or even surprise at various accounts we considered that vividly portrayed acts of racial and social injustice against African Americans. And then there was Tom, the jokester whose indiscreet, often rash, comments betrayed a privileged and perhaps somewhat pampered life; Bob, a nonstop talker who could scarcely contain his enthusiasm for each topic; and, finally, Jim, the quiet thinker.

One non–Talk Day, I was surprised at the following conversation. Slipping into my mother's distinctive, presumably Ozark, dialect, I instructed, "Let's clean up, y'all." My vocabulary included curiosities such as anti gogglin, dad gummit, and picayune, all phrases I assumed were indicative of my parent's southwest Missouri roots.

"Mrs. Fisher. Use proper English! You sound like a Texan," concluded Bob as he shut down his laptop.

---

1. The names of all students have been changed for confidentiality.

"Hey, that's a stereotype . . . isn't it?" remarked Yolanda trying to apply what had earlier been discussed in class. She eyed me cautiously waiting for my remark.

"Is it?" I countered.

"Well, Bob implied that all Texans speak like you just did. That is a stereotype." The conversation among the children continued as they filed out the classroom for their next subject.

As the year drew to a close, the students completed a written survey regarding Talk Day. Did I find that authentic discussions based on factual information promoted a personal awareness of stereotypes and racial issues? Definitely. Each student enjoyed Talk Days, identified personal stereotypes and those used by others, and became aware of actions stemming from stereotypes. Yolanda wrote, "[Understanding stereotypes] makes me move forward and get to really know other people better, instead of being put off by 'weird' dress or behavior. Who knows, they could turn out to be my best friend."

One of the deepest lessons I believe my students have learned has to do with the power of conversation. My students were able to talk about difficult and sometimes uncomfortable realities. Inequalities built around race, religion, gender, and other distinctions are often pervasive, but typically obscure, and students can benefit from seeking to take their measure. These steps can help:

- Talk with students, don't lecture them. Help them find their voice.
- Work across the curriculum. Diversity is a big topic that can reach across various subject areas and ties them together in powerful ways.
- Connect outside the classroom. The relevance of race, ethnicity, and gender can be witnessed daily, whether the perspective is global, local, or personal.

If conversations are both honest and respectful, we can deepen our understanding of both self and others. But if the toughest or most sensitive topics are "off-limits" or given shallow treatment, students will have little faith in the power of open inquiry and clear thinking to chip away at our intractable problems. I haven't created global harmony, but my students' eyes have been opened.

TEN

Educators Should Use Real-Life Examples to Teach About Prejudice

Mara Sapon-Shevin

> Mara Sapon-Shevin is a professor of inclusive education at Syracuse University. In this viewpoint she discusses the importance of recognizing opportunities to turn negative situations related to discrimination and prejudice into teachable moments. She brings forth the idea that prejudice is an inevitable component of the classroom due to the diversity of students. Sapon-Shevin believes instructors must take advantage of classroom occurrences involving prejudice and use those incidents to teach against discrimination.

A teacher approaches me in tears; there have been repeated racial incidents on her school's playground and she feels an urgent need to engage students in discussion and action related to creating safe schools and accepting communities. But when she brings this imperative to the school administrators, she is reminded that the statewide standardized tests are coming up soon and there simply isn't time to address these issues with students. She is told that she must concentrate exclusively on academic achievement so that the school will look good on the tests and not risk funding cuts or negative publicity. Her attempts to explain

Mara Sapon-Shevin, "Teachable Moments for Social Justice," in *Holding Values: What We Mean by Progressive Education*, ed. Brenda S. Engel with Anne C. Martin. Oxford: Heinemann, 2005.

the relationship between students' sense of safety and belonging and achievement scores are dismissed as interesting but not compelling.

The diversity of students in today's schools and the ways in which poverty, racism and violence creep—and sometimes stomp—into our classrooms presents a host of challenges for teachers. How do we create classroom climates that embody equity, social justice, inclusion and diversity while still achieving high "academic" standards? If the pressures of multiple agendas were not enough to leave us depleted and overwhelmed, the growing focus (one might say manic emphasis) on high stakes standardized testing has left many progressive educators even more frustrated. How do we maintain our focus on democratic, child-centered education in the face of a system that tells us that test scores are all that matters, and that there isn't enough time to pursue what are often labeled "soft" or secondary educational goals like classroom community or a commitment to ending racism and other oppressions?

"Teachable Moments" Are Everywhere

To some, making a commitment to social justice means that we must add a whole new "program" to an already overcrowded curriculum. In reality, however, there are "teachable moments" for social justice *everywhere* and a teacher who is primed and committed to noticing and responding to such moments can infuse values about belonging, right treatment and justice throughout the day. Consider, for example, what teaching opportunities are provided by the following situations:

- A fifth-grade boy draws swastikas on the paper of the only Jewish girl in the class.
- As they do their seatwork, students are pulling up the sides of their eyes to look "Asian" and chanting a rhyme about Japanese and Chinese people.
- A ninth-grader is slammed against the locker in the hallway and told he is a "stupid little faggot" and he better watch where he walks.

- As a teacher constructs her birthday chart and discusses how they will celebrate birthdays in her class, a young boy raises his hand and explains that he's not allowed to celebrate birthdays and another girl says that she heard that people from Africa sometimes don't know when their birthdays are and wonders how they celebrate.

All of the above are real incidents, and no doubt teachers can think of many more within their own classrooms and schools. The

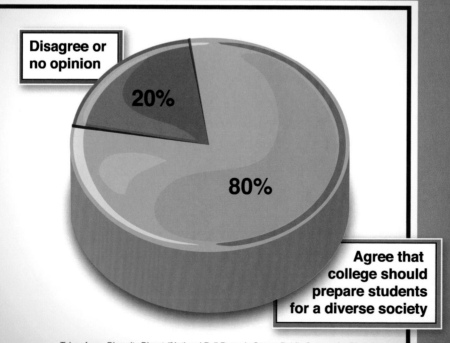

Education Should Prepare Students for a Diverse World

A recent survey of 2,011 Americans showed support for diversity curriculum in higher education, despite some recent negative media attention on the issue. The survey found that "80 percent of those polled agreed that 'it is just as important for colleges to prepare people to succeed in a diverse world as it is to prepare people with technical or academic skills.'"

Disagree or no opinion

20%

80%

Agree that college should prepare students for a diverse society

Taken from: *Diversity Digest*, "National Poll Reveals Strong Public Support for Diversity in Higher Education," 2008. www.diversityweb.org/digest/F98/publicsupport.html.

challenge is to respond to these in productive, educative ways that help all of us move towards a more inclusive and diverse society rather than letting them go by, either because we don't notice them or because we feel inadequate to respond or too rushed to prioritize such efforts. I have categorized teachable moments for social justice into two groups: *seized* and *lost*. For the last five years I have asked my pre-service teacher education students to document teachable moments for social justice they have seen in their own classrooms, heightening their awareness of both good teaching and encouraging them to observe the conditions of schools and classrooms that make responding productively more or less likely.

Teachers Can Make a Difference by Being Open and Ready

Being able to respond requires both noticing that the moment "happened" and having some responses ready. For example, after the September 11, 2001 attacks on the World Trade Center in New York City, a boy in one teacher's fifth grade class announced, "I think all Muslims should be sent back to their countries because they're all terrorists." The teacher, rather than criticizing the boy, engaged the class in a discussion. "Hmmm," she said, "I wonder how many of you remember the Oklahoma City bombing?" Many of the students raised their hands. "And who did it turn out was responsible for that?" she asked. "Timothy McVeigh" the students responded. "And what religion was he?" she persisted. "Catholic," they answered. "And how many of you are Catholic?" she asked her class, knowing the demographics already. Many hands went up. "Then I wonder if we should send all the Catholics in our class away because they might be dangerous terrorists." The students were shocked and protested, "Of course not, that was about him, not about being Catholic, that's not what they teach us at church" and on and on.

This teacher was able to challenge the dangerously problematic statement of a student by converting it to a powerful teachable moment about prejudice, stereotypes and over-generalization. Such lessons are precious and need to be actively encouraged.

We all need better repertoires of responding to oppressive behavior and language.

Sometimes our responses are inadequate because although we *noticed* the moment, we are unsure about how to respond. In one first grade classroom, students were drawing at their tables. One student looked over at another and said derisively, "You're Puerto Rican." The teacher, alert to the negative tone in the statement, responded quickly. "Don't say that!" and ended the conversation. Although she was, no doubt, responding to the pejorative tone with which the girl's ethnicity was mentioned, I worry that the message the students got was, "Don't talk about it"—don't notice or discuss people's differences in skin color, language or ethnicity. What would have had to be in place for the teacher to make another response? Perhaps to ask the "name calling" girl what she knows about Puerto Rico, or how she knows someone is Puerto Rican. Maybe the girl singled out, who was in fact Puerto Rican, might have been asked to share something of her own story at an appropriate moment.

How Can Teachers Be Prepared to Teach Against Stereotyping and Prejudice?

Our ability to respond constructively when teachable moments come up is not a simple matter. First, we must improve our sensitivity to the occurrence of the teaching occasion, our ability to "notice." This requires having a store of relevant information. We must know enough about Islam to be alert to other students' remarks about "starving" during Ramadan, or to students' confusion between religion, ethnicity, skin color and citizenship. Similarly, it will be hard to respond to the student who says that gay people caused AIDS if we don't [know] anything about the history of the disease or the ways in which it's spread. Simply put, we must learn more about different groups, about the ways in which oppression manifests itself, and about the occasions which might be problematic or occasion teasing, exclusion or mistreatment. Reading widely, talking to those outside our own group, pushing our own comfort level, asking respectful questions—these can all help us to get smarter about oppression. Maintaining an attitude of alertness is also critical: What are students saying to one another during work time? Who has no one to sit with at lunch? What was the fight on the playground about and how was it resolved? Although it is painful to notice things we feel powerless to change, *not* noticing gives students the message that oppression is inevitable and countering mistreatment hopeless. Even if we can do no more than notice and name the oppression, we model for students the powerful message that injustice is not invisible or acceptable.

Second, we must have structures and policies in place in our classrooms that make productive responses possible. After September 11, 2001, for example, teachers who had already established a strong classroom community found themselves better able to respond to the devastating tragedy and all the feelings and responses it provoked. Teachers who already had established a morning meeting and guidelines for community discussion, those who had started having their students keep journals, and schools that had a strong school-parent relationship were able to rally and respond more quickly. One elementary teacher who already had a word wall that included the words "prejudice," "discrimination," and "acceptance," was able to refer to those words when discussing the targeting of Arabs in the community and the importance of learning about others before jumping to conclusions. In classrooms that begin with an individual check-in for each student, teachers are more likely to be able to take the temperature of their class's social climate and have ways to respond.

Third, teachers need to develop repertoires for responding to social justice moments. Some of these responses are invariably reactive—we don't know that something will happen until it does. But sometimes sensitive teachers can predict that various experiences or processes will demand social justice teaching and do so proactively. For example, when one teacher's class was about to visit an old age home to interact with the residents, she engaged them in lengthy lessons on how to introduce themselves, how people's abilities to speak and hear may be impaired with age and how to respond respectfully and thoughtfully, and what it means to treat *all* people with dignity. The teacher's ability to prevent

The challenge for teachers in teaching diversity is to create a climate that promotes equity, social justice, and diversity, while maintaining high academic standards.

certain kinds of negative behavior was a function of her careful preparation of her students for the experience they were about to have. Teachers whose classrooms include students with a wide range of skills and abilities have unique opportunities to teach about individual differences, how and when to help one another, and what it means to be a community. This kind of preparation is far preferable to saying nothing and then needing to respond to comments like "You're stupid 'cause you read baby books," or "People who drool are disgusting!"

When our responses are commonly reactive, we need to know other ways that are age-appropriate and educative rather than punitive. The teacher responding to the statement about expelling all the Muslims was able to connect her students to their own experience in a way that was immediately transparent to them. In a second grade classroom, students started laughing about a story in which a child's letter to her grandma ended with X's and O's (symbolizing kisses and hugs). The teacher was able to move beyond the students' negative reaction to the idea of two women expressing that kind of affection to one another, and connect their discomfort to experiences in their own lives in which affection or physical contact was constrained or ridiculed. One might predict that her discussion about all the ways people show love, and differences between various families, cultures and situations, laid important, early groundwork for future discussions about how people are often teased or harassed for their sexual orientation or the way in which they express their sexuality.

Lastly, we must continually renew our own personal commitment to counteracting racism, homophobia, classism, and other forms of oppression and work hard to encourage one another—that is, to give one another courage—to act decisively even when we feel inadequate to the task.

The struggle to create and nurture democratic, inclusive schools and classrooms requires great fortitude and resilience. Many current educational initiatives are directly incompatible with fostering children's individual differences and the formation of cohesive, supportive learning communities. We need to share with one another our successes and our failures in working for social justice and learn how to support each other as we work to create schools and communities of justice and peace.

ELEVEN

Affirmative Action Programs Harm Minorities

Garin Hovannisian

> Garin Hovannisian is a graduate of the University of California at Los Angeles and the Columbia University Graduate School of Journalism. His writing has appeared in *The Los Angeles Times* and *The Christian Science Monitor*. In the following article he argues that affirmative action programs do not provide equality and actually hurt minorities by assuming that minorities cannot compete equally with whites.

As the lights change in front of me, I start to walk across Sunset Boulevard where I begin my daily journey to class. But instead of staring at the ground, thinking deep thoughts—a habit that I have most unfortunately developed over time—I look to my left, where I see in clear view a living incarnation of justice.

The cars that have stopped at the red light are as follows: a beautiful Rolls Royce, an exhausted Honda and a BMW. And their drivers, respectively: a middle-aged blonde woman, a white college student and an elderly black man. I see them stopped—the rich and the poor, the black and the white, the man and the woman. The light doesn't care. At that moment, the law is clear and everyone is equal under it.

Garin Hovannisian, "Affirmative Action Hurts Minorities," *Daily Bruin*, November 5, 2003. Reproduced by permission.

On the other side of the street, at UCLA [University of California at Los Angeles], reality gets a hold of me. It is "National Take Affirmative Action Day" and, in anachronistic fashion, a group of students denies what I have just seen: an equal, objective view of the world.

Affirmative Action Is Ineffective

Indeed, for most advocates of affirmative action, facts have little to do with convictions. After all, the effects of affirmative action on minority communities have been unhealthy at best. Thomas

Students at the University of California at Berkeley protest the passing of Proposition 209, which caused admission rates for minorities to fall.

Sowell, a scholar and economist at the Hoover Institution, writes, "What of the idea that affirmative action has helped blacks rise out of poverty and is needed to continue that rise? A far higher proportion of blacks in poverty rose out of poverty in the 20 years between 1940 and 1960—that is, before any major federal civil rights legislation—than in the more than 40 years since then." Similarly, in their book "America in Black and White," Stephan and Abigail Thernstrom confirm this. They write, "The growth of the black middle class long predates the adoption of race-conscious social policies."

When the use of affirmative action in the California college admissions process was blocked by Proposition 209, minority admission rates to the prominent University of California, Berkeley campus fell. But what is often neglected is that minority admission rates at less prominent UC [University of California] campuses actually went up even more. According to the UC Office of the President, the UC system admitted roughly 2,000 more minorities in 2002 than it did in 1997.

Do note, furthermore, that the "minorities" in question are artificially defined by the university. Armenians and Egyptians—indeed all Middle Easterners—fall under "white" and Chinese, Japanese and Korean students all fall under "Asian." But is the same courtesy extended to the diverse nationalities of black and Latino people? No. The foul fact is that, by politicizing the English language, university statistics undermine the true diversity of our campuses.

Linguistics aside, Proposition 209 has had a positive impact on minorities. By matching their abilities with the standards of their college, it has allowed minorities to compete and thrive. According to *Capitalism Magazine*, "At UC San Diego, in the year before Proposition 209's implementation, only one black freshman had a GPA [grade point average] of 3.5 or better." Compare this to 20 percent of white students. The reason is that the black students who could compete at San Diego were foolishly accepted by UCLA and Berkeley.

ADMISSIONS

IT'S HIS FAULT!

DAUGHTER of ALUM | SON of BIG DONOR | SOCCER PLAYER | RAISED in DISTANT STATE | MINORITY | DIDN'T GET IN

In 1998, as soon as affirmative action was derailed, 20 percent of black freshmen at UCSD [University of San Diego] had a 3.5 GPA. Yet we frequently hear that affirmative action is simply a program that levels the playing field between minorities and non-minorities.

Affirmative Action Is Harmful for Many Minorities

But to arrive at this conclusion is to accept its necessary pre-requisite: that minorities are incapable of competing with non-minorities; that they are intellectually inferior to them. The rebuttal that affirmative action tries to help those from poorer or disadvantaged backgrounds doesn't fly either. It is understand-able why a university might pick a financially troubled student over a financially advantaged student of equal merit. It is harder to achieve a level of academic success if you had to work three jobs to pay the rent. But affirmative action has nothing to do with promoting based on needs and everything to do with pro-moting based on race.

In allowing advocates of affirmative action to shape the struc-ture of the debate, we have lost sight of what the argument is all about. It isn't about the results of or the need for affirmative action. It isn't even about "white privilege" (I'm still waiting for mine to kick in) or racism. It is about whether affirmative action is right.

Close to 150 years ago, Frederick Douglass proclaimed to a group of abolitionists: "What I ask for the negro is not benevolence, not pity, not sympathy, but simply justice. The American people have always been anxious to know what they shall do with us. . . . I have had but one answer from the beginning. Do nothing with us!"

Affirmative action is not only ineffective, outdated, insulting, and racist but it is also wrong. Frederick Douglass, then Booker T. Washington, then Martin Luther King Jr. understood this. Justice isn't about preferences or condescension. It is about human liberty, equality and a struggle for success—not for the white race or the black race, but for the human race.

TWELVE

Affirmative Action Programs Result in Better Schools

Lee C. Bollinger

> Lee C. Bollinger is the president of Columbia University. In the following article he argues that affirmative action is a valuable and necessary tool to ensure diversity in higher education. Bollinger notes affirmative action is under attack, and some states have banned it entirely.

The admissions process has less to do with rewarding each student's past performance—although high performance is clearly essential—than it does with building a community of diverse learners who will thrive together and teach one another.

Racial Prejudice Is Still an Issue

When it comes to creating the kinds of diversity we sorely need in this country, however, disturbing trends and setbacks are making it difficult for many public schools and universities to succeed. The reality is that as much as we may want to believe that racial prejudice is a relic of history, conscience and experience tell us better. . . .

According to the 2000 census, only 14 percent of white students attend multiracial schools, while nearly 40 percent of both black and Latino students attend intensely segregated schools where 90 percent to 100 percent are from minority groups. Further, almost

Lee C. Bollinger, "Why Diversity Matters," *Education Digest*, vol. 73, October 2007, pp. 26–29. Reproduced by permission.

half of all black and Latino students attend schools where three-quarters or more students are poor, compared with only 5 percent of white students; in extremely poor schools, 80 percent of the students are black and Latino.

Beyond elementary and secondary schools, higher education continues to face its own challenges, including statewide bans on affirmative action. Recent news reports have noted how hard some of our leading public universities are working to revise recruitment and admissions policies to comply with those bans without jeopardizing the diversity of the students who attend their campuses. What's important, however, is why those universities are trying so hard to maximize diversity—even though no law requires it, and in several states affirmative action is explicitly forbidden.

I have been deeply involved in two U.S. Supreme Court cases—*Gratz v. Bollinger* and *Grutter v. Bollinger* (2003)—that ultimately upheld the constitutionality of affirmative-action policies at public universities. Let me suggest why, having vindicated the legality of affirmative action, higher education must not lose the practical and political battles to maintain racially, ethnically, and socioeconomically diverse student bodies.

Obligation to All Students

Universities understand that to remain competitive, their most important obligation is to determine—and then deliver—what future graduates will need to know about their world and how to gain that knowledge. While the last century witnessed a new demand for specialized research, prizing the expert's vertical mastery of a single field, the emerging global reality calls for new specialists who can synthesize a diversity of fields and draw quick connections among them.

The experience of arriving on a campus to live and study with classmates from a diverse range of backgrounds is essential to students' training for this new world, nurturing in them an instinct to reach out instead of clinging to the comforts of what seems natural or familiar.

Segregation Still Exists in Public Schools

Schools all over the country remain highly segregated. Many educators support affirmative action programs that help create more diversity in education.

State	Percentage of black students in 90–100 percent of minority schools	State	Percentage of black students in majority white schools
Michigan	62.5%	New York	13.6%
New York	60.8%	California	14.1%
Illinois	60.1%	Michigan	17.6%
New Jersey	50.0%	Illinois	18.2%
Maryland	50.0%	Maryland	21.3%
Pennsylvania	48.3%	Mississippi	22.6%
Alabama	43.1%	Louisiana	23.1%
Wisconsin	42.9%	New Jersey	24.3%
Louisiana	42.2%	Texas	24.3%
Mississippi	41.3%	Wisconsin	27.1%
California	37.1%	Georgia	27.7%
Texas	37.0%	Connecticut	28.2%
Missouri	36.2%	Pennsylvania	28.9%
Georgia	35.4%	Ohio	29.4%
Ohio	35.1%	Alabama	29.6%
Connecticut	32.2%	Missouri	32.5%
Florida	30.6%	Massachusetts	32.5%
Massachusetts	24.6%	Arkansas	32.7%
Indiana	21.3%	Rhode Island	35.4%
Colorado	20.0%	Florida	35.6%

Taken from: Civil Rights Project, "A Multiracial Society with Segregated Schools: Are We Losing the Dream?" Harvard University, January 2003.

The college experience of living and studying with classmates of diverse backgrounds is essential in preparing students to function in a diverse world without prejudices.

Affirmative-action programs help achieve that larger goal. And the universities that create and carry them out do so not only because overcoming longstanding obstacles to people of color and women in higher education is the right thing to do, but also because policies that encourage a comprehensive diversity help universities achieve their mission. Specifically, they are indispensable in training future leaders how to lead all of society, and by attracting a diverse cadre of students and faculty, they increase our universities' chances of filling in gaps in our knowledge with research and teaching on a wider—and often uncovered—array of subjects.

Choosing the Best Applicants Is Complicated

Opponents of affirmative action forget that broader purpose in their demand for what they see as a "pure" admissions meritocracy based on how students perform in high school and on standardized tests. But it is far less important to reward past performance—and impossible to isolate a candidate's objective talent from the contextual realities shaping that performance—than to make the best judgment about which applicants can contribute to help form the strongest class that will study and live together.

For graduate schools and employment recruiters, that potential is the only "merit" that matters, because in an increasingly global world, it is impossible to compete without already knowing how to imagine, understand, and collaborate with a diverse and fluid set of colleagues, partners, customers, and government leaders.

Affirmative Action Increases Diversity

By abolishing all public affirmative-action programs, voters in California and Michigan (and other states if affirmative-action opponents are successful) have not only toppled a ladder of equal opportunity in higher education that so many of us fought to build and the Supreme Court upheld in 2003. They will almost assuredly make their great public universities less diverse—and have, in fact, done so in California, where the impact has become clear—and therefore less attractive options to potential students and, ultimately, less valuable contributors to our globalized society.

As the president of a private university, I am glad that independent institutions retain the autonomy to support diversity efforts that make our graduates more competitive candidates for employers and graduate schools, as well as better informed citizens in our democracy and the world. But as an alumnus of one public university and a former president of another, I worry about a future in which one of America's great success stories slides backward from the mission of providing generations of young Americans with access to an affordable higher education.

From the establishment of the land-grant colleges in the 1860s to the GI Bill [that provided education benefits for veterans] after World War II to the Higher Education Act of 1965, our public universities have advanced the notion that in educating college students for the world they will inhabit, it is necessary to bring people together from diverse parts of society and to educate them in that context. Far from being optional or merely enriching, it is the very essence of what we mean by a liberal or humanistic education.

It is also vital for establishing a cohesive, truly national society—one in which rising generations learn to overcome the biases they absorb as children while also appreciating the unique talents their colleagues bring to any equation. Only education can get us there.

As Justice Thurgood Marshall knew so well: "The legal system can open doors and sometimes even knock down walls. But it cannot build bridges. . . . We will only attain freedom if we learn to appreciate what is different and muster the courage to discover what is fundamentally the same." Cutting affirmative action short now only betrays that history of social progress. And, in the process, it threatens the core value of academically renowned public universities at a time when many Americans list rising tuition costs as one of their gravest economic concerns.

All of this leads to the conclusion that diversity—one of the great strengths of American education—is under siege today. At the elementary- and secondary-school levels, resegregation is making it exceedingly difficult for minority students to get the resources that inspire rising generations to apply to and then attend college. At the same time, the elimination of affirmative-action programs at our public universities is keeping admissions officials from lifting those same students up to offset the structural inequalities they had to face in getting there.

As we honor the parents, students, lawyers, and nine justices who spoke with one voice in *Brown* [*v. the Board of Education of Topeka*, which overturned segregation laws] on that May day 53 years ago, we would all do well to remember that when it comes to responsible diversity programs—those that help our public schools and our great public universities fulfill their historic roles as avenues of economic and cultural mobility—what is wise is also what is just.

"We will only attain freedom if we learn to appreciate what is different and muster the courage to discover what is fundamentally the same."

THIRTEEN

Legislation Is Needed to Help Fight Violence Based on Prejudice

Julian Bond and Wade Henderson

> Julian Bond is the chairman of the National Association for the Advancement of Colored People (NAACP), and Wade Henderson is the president of the Leadership Conference on Civil Rights. In the following article they point to a recent rise in the number of hate crimes and argue for national legislation to help prevent this violent discrimination.

Last April [2006] David Ritcheson testified before a House Judiciary Committee panel about how he had been beaten, burned and sodomized by self-styled skinheads who were shouting anti-Hispanic slurs.

Ritcheson never recovered from the traumatizing attack, and, only two months after his congressional testimony, he committed suicide. He was only 18. His personal tragedy—and the plight of thousands of other Americans who are attacked every year because of their race, religion, gender, disability, national origin or sexual identity—should push the House [of Representatives] to vote on a bill to enact national legislation against hate crimes.

Two concerns may cause strong supporters of civil rights to hesitate before supporting hate crimes legislation. Because of its legislative history, it has become part of the Department of

Julian Bond and Wade Henderson, "The Need for a Law Against Hate Crimes," *The Hill*, December 6, 2007. Reproduced by permission.

Defense authorization bill. Therefore, civil rights supporters who fervently oppose the Iraq war may also vote against the entire defense bill, including the hate crimes law. We understand their concerns; one of us was expelled from the Georgia legislature for opposing the Vietnam War. But the fate of the Defense authorization bill will not determine the length of the war in Iraq; it will decide the future of the fight against hate crimes.

On the other side of the spectrum, some have contended that the hate crimes law will prevent religious leaders from preaching against practices they oppose. But the hate crimes law punishes

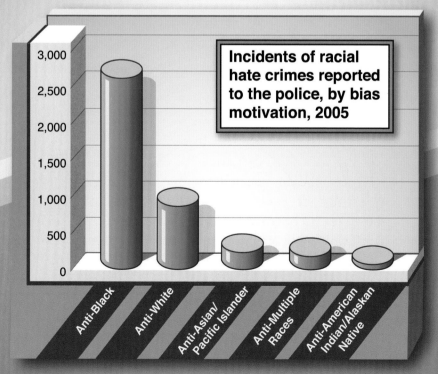

Racial Hate Crimes by Motivation

Statistics from the Federal Bureau of Investigation show that racial hate crimes are a serious problem in the United States.

Incidents of racial hate crimes reported to the police, by bias motivation, 2005

Taken from: Federal Bureau of Investigation, "Hate Crimes Statistics, 2005," Uniform Crime Reports.

violence that results in death or bodily injury, not the exercise of free speech. Make no mistake—the issue is physical attacks, not religious doctrines.

As the FBI [Federal Bureau of Investigation] recently reported, nearly 10,000 Americans were the targets of hate crimes last year [2006], an 8 percent increase from 2005.

That's bad enough, but the real number of hate crime victims is almost certainly much larger. Many state and local governments don't collect data on hate crimes, and many incidents of violence motivated by bigotry are not reported.

National Legislation Is Necessary

That is why it is so important that both houses of Congress pass the Local Law Enforcement Hate Crimes Prevention Act and place it on President [George W.] Bush's desk. The law takes two actions that are long-overdue: Making clear that victims of hate crimes based on their gender, sexual orientation, disability or gender identity should be protected under federal law. And helping states that need more resources to fight hate crimes, including states that have failed to act in the past.

Hate crimes should be something we learn about in history books, but, tragically, we can still read about them in our daily newspapers. The gruesome murder of a young, gay, African American man in West Virginia, the appearance of nooses in the nation's high schools and colleges, and the growing numbers of attacks against immigrants, gays and lesbians all remind us that this is a national problem that requires national action.

Some ask why it is necessary to distinguish between hate crimes and other, equally loathsome, incidents. Here's the truth—hate crimes don't just target individuals; they attack the very idea of America as a blessed land with liberty and justice for all. When people are singled out because of who they are, how they worship, how they live, or where their families came from, entire communities can be torn apart by fear and rage. Moreover, hate-

Longtime civil rights advocate and viewpoint coauthor Julian Bond argues that national hate crimes legislation is needed to prevent violent discrimination against minorities.

ful words can wound people as much as fists, knives and even bullets. Moreover, imagine an elderly woman who survived the Holocaust being mugged outside her home as her attacker shouts anti-Semitic slurs that bring back terrible memories of the horrors she endured more than 60 years ago; targeted yet again, because of her faith.

For almost 10 years, the Congress has put off taking action against the violence that targets the vulnerable, tears apart our communities, and makes a mockery of America's finest, founding ideals.

Now is the time for the House to take a stand against the hate crimes that marred our nation's last two centuries and have no place in 21st-century America.

What You Should Know About Prejudice

Discrimination and intolerance stem from a variety of motivations: racial prejudice, gender prejudice, religious prejudice, prejudice against certain sexual orientations, prejudice against people with disabilities, and prejudice against certain family structures, among others.

Prejudice Based on Gender

The Equal Pay Act of 1963 requires that men and women be given equal pay for equal work in the same establishment:

- Employers may not pay unequal wages to men and women who perform jobs that require substantially equal skill, effort, and responsibility and that are performed under similar working conditions within the same establishment.
- Pay differentials are permitted when they are based on seniority, merit, quantity or quality of production, or a factor other than sex.

Still, in 2005, women earned only seventy-seven cents for every dollar earned by men. This wage gap was more significant for minority groups, with African American women earning seventy-one cents per dollar earned by men and Latinas earning fifty-eight cents for every dollar earned by men.

Prejudice Based on Race

Title VII of the Civil Rights Act of 1964 protects individuals against employment discrimination on the basis of race, skin color, and national origin, among other things. The legislation:

- Prohibits discrimination against any employee or job applicant in regard to hiring, termination, promotion, compensation, job training, or any other term, condition, or privilege of employment.
- Prohibits employment decisions based on stereotypes and assumptions about abilities, traits, qualities, or performance.
- Prohibits harassment on the basis of race and color. Ethnic slurs, racial "jokes," offensive or derogatory comments, or other verbal or physical conduct based on an individual's race or color constitutes unlawful harassment, especially if the conduct creates an intimidating, hostile, or offensive working environment, or interferes with the individual's work performance.
- Prohibits segregation and classification of employees.

However, in fiscal year 2007, the U.S. Equal Employment Opportunity Commission received 30,510 charges of race discrimination. From 2003 to 2007, the American-Arab Anti-Discrimination Committee received about ten reports of employment discrimination against Arab Americans each week.

Prejudice Based on Sexual Orientation

Executive order 13087 of 1998 prohibits discrimination based on sexual orientation within the federal civilian workforce. But no federal laws protect citizens from discrimination based on sexual orientation in the larger workforce. Some state and local governments have laws in place to protect against this type of discrimination.

As with prejudice in general, sexual orientation discrimination is prevalent in schools and a factor in many incidents of bullying.

- In U.S. schools, 75 percent of students are not protected by laws against harassment or discrimination based on their sexual orientation.

• Ninety-seven percent of students in the U.S. report regularly hearing homophobic remarks in school.

Hate Crimes

Crimes that are motivated by prejudice may be considered in the context of hate crime laws:

• The Violent Crime Control and Law Enforcement Act of 1994 requires the United States Sentencing Commission (USSC) to increase the penalties for federal crimes committed on the basis of perceived race, color, religion, national origin, ethnicity, gender, disability, or sexual orientation.

• Title 18 makes it unlawful to injure, intimidate, or interfere with any person's attempt to engage in certain federal activities—such as attending public school, serving on a jury, voting, engaging in employment, or traveling across state lines—based on that person's race, color, religion, or national origin. Persons violating this statute may be federally prosecuted and subject to civil and/or criminal penalties.

In 2006, the Federal Bureau of Investigation identified 9,652 victims of hate crimes. Fifty-two percent of those were victims of racial prejudice, 15 percent were victims of sexual orientation prejudice, and 14 percent were victims of prejudice against their ethnicity or national origin.

What You Should Do About Prejudice

Whether prejudice is innate or learned or some combination of both, most people agree that it can and should be reduced. Be aware of prejudice and stereotyping in your family or among your friends. Talk about these issues with your parents and peers. Most likely, you will have exposure to some kind of diversity education at school. Ask questions of your teachers, and think about your own conscious and even subconscious prejudices. If you do have a diversity program at your school, ask about computer programs that can help you become aware of subconscious prejudices you might hold.

Talk to Your Parents and Friends

Because talking about prejudices can increase awareness, address prejudice directly when you hear it or see it. Many times, people are not even aware that they are discriminating against someone. Talking about prejudice with your parents and peers can help them and you.

If, however, you witness violent prejudiced behavior, do not try to confront the violent person. Talk to your parents or teachers who can help you report the behavior to the proper authorities. Laws protect people from these kinds of behaviors. For example, people can be prosecuted for hate crimes or bias-motivated crimes.

Do Your Research

Prejudice can often stem from unfamiliarity; if we are not exposed to certain groups of people, it is easy to make assumptions and develop stereotypes about those groups. Reading about prejudice and discrimination can help you understand your biases. Novels and short stories written by and about groups you are unfamiliar with can help you begin to understand what the experiences of others are like. Talk to your teachers to see if they can recommend readings to you. Finally, visit the Web. Many organizations work to reduce prejudice and discrimination in the United States, and they provide helpful information on their Web sites.

Examine Your Own Views

Once you have exposed yourself to these issues, it might be helpful to ask yourself some questions. These questions can help you eliminate both conscious and subconscious prejudice. What is your background? Which groups do you identify with? Do your parents talk to you about prejudice and discrimination? Have you ever hurt someone's feelings or avoided someone because he or she belonged to a particular group? Have you seen your friends discriminate against someone because of his or her race or social class? How did that make you feel? How did that person feel? Do you feel comfortable standing up to your friends about prejudice and discrimination?

Take a Stand

As you read the viewpoints in this book, think about the issues being raised. The readings in this volume are designed to make you think about prejudice and raise your awareness. As you come to know more about prejudice, you can make a difference by working to reduce prejudice in your own life.

Think about where you fit in and how you define yourself. Then, think about how you relate to others. If you are unhappy with the way you interact with people from different groups, do something about it. Try to talk to someone outside of your usual circle of friends. Try to think about what you can learn from the experiences of others.

Finally, stand up for what you think is right. As long as you are in a safe environment, respectfully address incidences of prejudice and discrimination that you witness. And of course, report any violent behavior to a trusted adult.

Anyone can make a difference when it comes to eliminating prejudice, whether it's changing one's own views or raising the awareness of others.

ORGANIZATIONS TO CONTACT

The editors have compiled the following list of organizations concerned with the issues debated in this book. The descriptions are derived from materials provided by the organizations. All have publications or information available for interested readers. The list was compiled on the date of publication of the present volume; the information provided here may change. Be aware that many organizations take several weeks or longer to respond to inquiries, so allow as much time as possible.

Anti-Defamation League (ADL)
823 United Nations Plaza, New York, NY 10017
(212) 885-7755 • Web site: www.adl.org

The ADL was founded in 1913 "to stop the defamation of the Jewish people and to secure justice and fair treatment to all." Now it is the nation's premier civil rights/human relations agency. The ADL today fights anti-Semitism and all forms of bigotry, defends democratic ideals, and protects civil rights for all people. The league publishes annual reports and online newsletters to inform the public of the status of hate in America and the league's efforts to fight it.

Center for Democratic Renewal (CDR)
PO Box 50469, Atlanta, GA 30302
(404) 221-0025 • Web site: www.publiceye.org/cdr/cdr.html
e-mail: cdr@igc.apc.org

The CDR is a multiracial organization working to advance the vision for a democratic and diverse society free of racism and bigotry. This community-based coalition fights hate group activity. The center's publications include *When Hate Groups Come to Town*, which is intended to guide individuals and communities to respond safely and effectively to resulting violence.

Center for Equal Opportunity

815 Fifteenth St. NW, Ste. 928, Washington, DC 20005
(202) 639-0803 • Web site: www.ceousa.org

The Center for Equal Opportunity is a nonprofit organization that supports research and publishes policy briefs on issues related to race, ethnicity, and public policy. The center's particular areas of focus include affirmative action, immigration and assimilation, and bilingual education. The center's Web site gives access to the Anti-Discrimination Hotline, which exists to monitor cases of "affirmative action" and "diversity" programs and to bring an end to these unequal opportunities.

Diversity Web

Web site: www.diversityweb.org

Diversity Web is a World Wide Web organization that focuses on diversity in higher education. Its Web site highlights three hundred schools in the United States that are working to make an institutional commitment to diversity on campuses. Selected publications are available on the Web site that highlight diversity plans and guides for American colleges and universities.

National Association for the Advancement of Colored People (NAACP)

4805 Mt. Hope Dr., Baltimore, MD 21215
(410) 358-8900 • Web site: www.naacp.org

The NAACP is one of the most prominent civil rights organizations in the country. The organization works to ensure the political, social, educational, and economic equality of all minority citizens in the United States. The NAACP's strategic plan is available for download on its Web site, along with education resources and advocacy tools.

National Council of La Raza (NCLR)

1111 Nineteenth St. NW, Ste. 1000, Washington, DC 20036
(202) 785-1670 • Web site: www.nclr.org

NCLR is an organization that works for the civil rights and economic opportunities of Hispanic Americans. The NCLR conducts applied research, policy analysis, and advocacy through community-based organizations. The council publishes reports that examine disaster management for immigrants, educational support for children, and election opportunities and results, among other things.

National Organization for Women (NOW)
1100 H St. NW, Third Fl., Washington, DC 20005
(202) 628-8669 • Web site: www.now.org

NOW is the largest, most comprehensive feminist advocacy group in the United States. Its purpose is to take action to bring women into full participation in society—sharing equal rights, responsibilities, and opportunities with men, while living free from discrimination. Among its many efforts, NOW works to secure reproductive and abortion rights for women and to end all forms of violence against women. The *National NOW Times* covers a range of women's issues and is available on the Web site.

National Urban League
120 Wall St., New York, NY 10005
(212) 558-5300 • Web site: www.nul.org

The National Urban League is a social service and civil rights organization. It works to assist African Americans in the achievement of social and economic equality. The league promotes empowerment through education, economic self-sufficiency, health, leadership, and racial justice. *Opportunity Journal* and *Urban Influence Magazine* examine and inform the continuing civil rights movement.

The United States Gay and Lesbian United Front
13377 Wardlow Rd., Sardinia, OH 45171
Web site: http://timlonaker.com

The United States Gay and Lesbian United Front is a nonprofit organization that works to make sure that gay, lesbian, bisexual, and transgender persons are elected to the U.S. House of Representatives and the Senate and included in their chosen communities of faith. The organization also works to disseminate the latest news on marriage equality.

BIBLIOGRAPHY

Books

Theodore Dalrymple, *In Praise of Prejudice*. New York: Encounter, 2007.

Tish Davidson, *Prejudice*. Danbury, CT: Scholastic, 2003.

bell hooks, *Feminism Is for Everybody*. Cambridge, MA: South End, 2000.

Clarence B. Jones, *What Would Martin Say?* New York: HarperCollins, 2008.

Frances E. Kendall, *Understanding White Privilege*. Oxford: Taylor & Francis, 2006.

Jonathan Kozol, *Savage Inequalities: Children in America's Schools*. New York: Harper Perennial, 1992.

Barack Obama, *Dreams from My Father: A Story of Race and Inheritance*. New York: Three Rivers, 2004.

Paula Rothenberg, *Race, Class, and Gender in the United States*. New York: Worth, 2006.

Barbara Trepagnier, *Silent Racism: How Well-Meaning White People Perpetuate the Racial Divide*. Boulder, CO: Paradigm, 2007.

Periodicals

Robert Azzi, "Deconstructing 'the Other'—and Ourselves," *Nieman Reports*, Summer 2007.

Siri Carpenter, "Buried Prejudice," *Scientific American*, 2008.

Dave Clark, "Political Bias," *Inc.*, March 2008.

Community Care, "The Big? Is Society Prejudiced Against Disabled People?" December 2006.

Barbara Ehrenreich, "All-American Anti-Semitism," *Progressive*, February 2007.

Michael Fitzpatrick, "Obesity Crusade Is a Triumph of Prejudice over Evidence," *Community Care*, November 2007.

David Glenn, "Our Hidden Prejudices, on Trial," *Chronicle of Higher Education*, April 2008.

Sally Lehrman, "Make Diversity a Curriculum Core," *Quill*, August 2007.

Michael Nelson, "Stereotype, Then and Now," *Chronicle of Higher Education*, October 2007.

Thomas Pack, "Test Your Prejudices Online," *Information Today*, March 2007.

John Ridley, "The New Bigotry," *Esquire*, June 2008.

William Stewart, "'Blown Away' by Class Prejudice," *Times Educational Supplement*, February 2008.

Shawn T. Taylor, "Battling Bias," *Essence*, April 2007.

Gary Younge, "Jena Is America," *Nation*, October 2007.